Puss in Boots

A Pantomime

Norman Robbins

CW00550384

Samuel French - London
New York - Toronto - Hollywood

CHARACTERS

In order of appearance

Mother Goose, Fairy Godmother to all
Marjory Daw
Jack Spratt
Caspar ⎫
Hector ⎭ the Miller's lazy sons
Peter, their younger brother
Puss, his only friend
Gruesome, the Ogre's henchman
Fanny the Fifth, Queen of Arcadia
The Lord Chamberlain
Freckles, a page
Princess Miranda
Crunchbones, the Ogre

Chorus of Villagers, Gypsies, Fairies, Demons, etc.

SYNOPSIS OF SCENES

ACT I

ACT II

MUSICAL NUMBERS

Please read the note on page vi

ACT I
No. 1   Villagers
No. 2   Jack, Marjory
No. 3   Peter
No. 4   Freckles, Children
Dance   Gypsies
No. 5   Queen, Chorus
No. 6   Princess
No. 7   Puss, Peter
No. 8   Dance: Jack, Marjory, Chorus
No. 9   Peter
No. 10   Company

ACT II
No. 11   Dance: Courtiers
No. 12   Princess, Peter
No. 13   Queen, Freckles
No. 14   Mother Goose, Puss
No. 15   Peter, Princess
No. 16   Freckles, Queen
No. 17   Cooks
No. 18   Company

MUSIC

The choice of songs is left to the individual director. Please read the notice below most carefully:

A licence issued by Samuel French Ltd to perform this play does NOT include permission to use any copyright music in the performance. The notice printed below on behalf of the Performing Right Society should be carefully read.

The following statement concerning the use of music is printed here on behalf of the Performing Right Society Ltd, by whom it was supplied

The permission of the owner of the performing right in copyright music must be obtained before any public performance may be given, whether in conjunction with a play or sketch or otherwise, and this permission is just as necessary for amateur performances as for professional. The majority of copyright musical works (other than oratorios, musical plays and similar dramatico-musical works) are controlled in the British Commonwealth by the PERFORMING RIGHT SOCIETY LTD, 29–33 BERNERS STREET, LONDON W1P 4AA.

The Society's practice is to issue licences authorizing the use of its repertoire to the proprietors of premises at which music is publicly performed, or, alternatively, to the organizers of musical entertainments, but the Society does not require payment of fees by performers as such. Producers or promoters of plays, sketches, etc., at which music is to be performed, during or after the play or sketch, should ascertain whether premises at which their performances are to be given are covered by a licence issued by the Society and, if they are not, should make application to the Society for particulars as to the fee payable.

AUTHOR'S NOTE

This pantomime was written at the request of the Palace Theatre, Newark, and presented there in January, 1992. When I sat down with Brien Chitty to discuss their requirements, they asked for a "Slosh" scene, and a U.V. one which at that time seemed no problem at all. When the actual writing began, however, I found myself in difficulties, for there was nowhere in the outlined plot where either could be placed . . . and in addition to this there was the problem of the Ogre's transformation from Giant to Lion and then to Mouse in full view of the audience. I solved the problem by lumping them all together in the final scene. Smugly depositing the completed script into the waiting hands of the Palace Theatre team, it suddenly struck me that should anyone else want to stage it, I'd given them a few problems. Many of the smaller societies did not have the facilities for the U.V. and transformation scene. A quick re-write made it possible for the U.V. scene to be lifted out without damaging continuity, and if yours is one of the societies who can't cope with . . . or don't want U.V. . . . here's the solution. Following the Ogre's line, "A laugh, eh? Then watch and I'll prove it to you." Puss says, "I shouldn't bother if I were you. I've seen it all before. There's nothing *you* can do that my master can't. He can even change his *shape*." Omit the Ogre's spell and U.V. scene, picking up on Ogre's line, "Bah . . . any magician can do that."

For the Ogre's transformation, Ogre speaks the spell. Lights fade quickly to black-out. Ogre exits. Lion enters. Lights go up. For the second change, following the speech, "You doubt my powers? Then watch." Lights fade quickly to black-out, Lion exits. Lights go back up. The next four lines are said as script then Puss says, "You must be a very small mouse. I can't even see you. You'll have to come closer." Ogre replies, "Oh, very well. Now can you see me?" then the rest is as script. Obviously there is no need for the audience to see the Mouse, and equally obvious is the fact that the Ogre's voice must be done on an offstage mic throughout for better effect.

Apart from that, producing societies should have no problems with the rest of the script. Keep songs bright and bouncy, costumes colourful and with a good pace to it all, everyone should enjoy themselves.

Norman Robbins

For

Ethel Clee
an inadequate thank you for
the pleasure your singing
gave to so many people in
so many wonderful Operettas.

PROLOGUE

Mother Goose's Arbor

There is a gauze lane-cloth which depicts a gigantic shimmering spider's web.
The Lights give the effect of early morning with, if possible, light mist

When the CURTAIN *rises, Mother Goose is standing* DC, *smiling. She is a*
motherly figure, middle-aged to elderly, dressed in the traditional costume of
the Nursery-Rhyme character and carries a wooden spoon which she uses as a
wand

Mother Goose (*cheerily*)   Thrice welcome to Arcadia . . .
A land untouched by time,
Where live those folk we know so well
From Fairy Tale and Nursery-Rhyme.
A magic place where strange adventures
Ev'ry day befall,
Yet thanks to me . . . no real harm comes
To anybody here at all. (*She smiles*)
What's that, you say? And who am I?
Why, bless my soul, my dears . . .
Don't tell me you've forgotten me?
I've known you all for *years*.
Mums and Dads . . . Grandparents too . . .
Oh, surely you recall?
I'm Mother Goose, as ever was,
The Fairy Godmother to all. (*She curtsies*)

Good gracious me. Fancy forgetting who I am. (*To someone in the front
row*) I'm surprised at *you*, my dear. When I think of the times I watched
over *you* when you were little . . . (*She chuckles*) But never mind . . .
There's no need to blush. Mortals always *did* tend to forget things as they
grew older. Here in Arcadia, of course, folk never *get* any older. That's
one of the best things about it. No matter how long it's been since you
visited us last, you'll always find us looking exactly the same. Still—you
haven't come here to listen to *me* chattering, have you? Of course not.
You want a story. Something to keep you amused for a while. Well—I've
got lots of stories up here, you know. (*She taps her temple gently*) There's
the one about . . . (*Stopping*) No. Not that one. You heard it *last* year,
didn't you? But there *is* the one about . . . (*Stopping again*) No. And that's
no use either. You must have heard it a dozen times. (*Frowning*) Well, I'll
be blessed. I've got so many tales in my head I can't think of a single one
to tell you. No, no, wait a minute, I'm wrong. I'll tell you a tale *about* a
tail. Or perhaps I *should* say—a creature *attached* to a tail. (*She beams*)

Oh, yes, it's the purr-fect story for tonight. You all like cats, don't you? Then I'll tell you the tale of *Puss in Boots*. So settle back in your seats whilst I wave my magic spoon and show you exactly what happened a few years ago right here in Arcadia. (*She flourishes her spoon*)

There is a flash

Mother Goose exits as:

The gauze lane-cloth opens

ACT I

SCENE 1

A village in Arcadia. It is a bright and sunny morning

A typical pantomime village setting of half-timbered cottages with thatched roofs against a backdrop of wooded hillsides and green fields. A small rustic bridge is UL and this leads away from the village. DL and DR are shops and houses to mask entrances and exits

The Villagers are singing and dancing exuberantly and it is obvious that all is right with the world

Song 1 (Villagers)

At the end of the song, Marjory Daw, a pretty young milk-maid hurries over the bridge and makes her way DC in a state of great excitement

Marjory (*breathlessly*) Listen, everyone. Listen. I've got the most awful news to tell you.

Everyone crowds around her

Boy (*stepping forward*) What is it, Marjory Daw? What's wrong?
Marjory It's the wickedest thing I've ever heard. You know the old Miller died last week without making a will, and we all thought his three sons would share everything between them?

All nod their agreement

Well today they did it—and you'll never *believe* what happened. Caspar has taken the Mill. Hector's claimed the donkey that carried the sacks— and poor Peter's been left with nothing but the old cat who's so toothless that he can't catch mice any more and spends the whole day sleeping.
Villagers (*murmuring disgustedly*) Shame. Disgraceful, (etc.).
Marjory But that's not the worst of it. Now they've turned him out of the house too, and told him to find somewhere else to live.

All react

Boy (*protesting*) They can't do *that*. Peter's got as much right to stay there as *they* have.

All agree

Girl (*indignantly*) *More*. He's the only one who helped his father grind the corn and weigh the flour into sacks. All *they* did was to make fun of him for working so hard. Poor Peter. Whatever is he going to do?

Marjory (*dejectedly*) I've no idea. Oh, if only Jack Spratt were here. I'm sure *he'd* do something.

Boy Yes, where *is* Jack Spratt? Has anyone seen him today?

Girl (*looking off* UR) Here he comes now.

Villagers (*cheering loudly*) Hooray.

Jack Spratt enters UR, *a dashing young man with a jaunty air. He moves* DC

Jack (*brightly*) Now that's what I *call* a welcome. Good-morning, everyone.

Marjory (*hurrying to him*) Oh, Jack, thank goodness you've arrived. Have you heard the awful news about Peter?

Jack (*cheerfully*) Yes, but don't worry. They won't get away with it. As soon as *I* found out, I went straight to the palace and spoke to the Lord Chamberlain. He's promised to tell the Queen everything, so don't be surprised if she comes here herself to sort things out. As you know—she simply hates people who cheat.

Girl (*awed*) The Queen? Coming here? (*Excitedly*) Oh, I must go and put my best dress on. I can't let her see me in *these* old things.

Girl 2 Nor me. And the boys can smarten *them*selves up, *too*. We don't want her to think we're peasants.

She grabs a boy's hand

Come on, Colin.

The Villagers exit quickly

Marjory (*adoringly*) Oh Jack, I *knew* you'd think of something to help him. And I can't wait to see if the Queen does come.

Jack (*smiling*) Well—I only said she might—but it would be nice if she did. (*Brightening*) She may even bring Princess Miranda with her. They do say she's the most beautiful girl in the whole of Arcadia.

Marjory (*put out*) *Do* they, indeed? (*She turns away from him*)

Jack (*quickly*) But of course, they haven't seen *you*, yet. And as far as I'm concerned, *you're* the prettiest girl in the whole wide world.

Marjory (*melting*) Oooh. Do you think so? Honest and truly? (*She turns back*)

Jack Honest and truly.

Song 2 (Jack and Marjory)

At the end of the song, Jack and Marjory exit happily DL, *as:*

Caspar and Hector enter over the bridge. They are an ill-matched couple, both somewhat short of intelligence and wearing garish-coloured clothes. They move down DC, *chuckling*

Caspar Just think, Hector. Everything that belonged to Dad now belongs to us.

Hector (*beaming*) Yeah, good job we found that will before anybody else saw it. (*Indignantly*) Fancy Dad leaving everything to Peter and nothing to us. Spiteful old thing.

Caspar Mind you—we've still got to be careful. (*He glances around furtively*) We could end up in jail if anybody found out the truth. That frosty faced Queen Fanny could make us hand it all back to him.

Hector How can she? Now we've kicked him out of the house, he's got nowhere to live, has he? By this time tomorrow he'll be miles away—and we can't give him everything back if we don't know where he is, can we? It stands to reason.

Caspar Maybe you're right—but just to be on the safe side, we'd better get rid of the evidence before anybody gets suspicious. Give me the will and I'll tear it up and throw it in the river. (*He holds out his hand*)

Hector What do you mean, give you the will? *I* ain't got it.

Caspar Eh?

Hector I said *I* ain't got it.

Caspar (*wincing*) What do you mean, you "ain't got it"? Where's your grammar?

Hector Gone to Bingo with me grandad.

Caspar (*pushing him*) Idiot. Don't you know *anything* about the English language? (*Patiently*) You *haven't* got the will. *I* haven't got the will. *They* haven't got the will. *He* hasn't got the will. *She* hasn't got the will.

Hector Blimey, who *has* got it then?

Caspar (*grabbing him*) Nobody's got it, you numbskull. You've *lost* it, haven't you? You've lost it. (*He pushes him away*) I should have known better than to trust you to look after it. Now we'll have to walk all the way back to the Mill to see if we can find it—and it's *two* miles. Two miles.

Hector So what? That's only a mile each

Caspar (*groaning*) Oooh, how can one person be so *stupid*?

Hector (*indignantly*) Here—who are you calling stupid? I've got more brains that you have.

Caspar That's a laugh. You can't even count up to ten.

Hector Yes, I can. (*He counts to ten*) See.

Caspar All right, clever-clogs. And what comes after ten?

Hector Er—Jack, Queen, King and Ace.

Caspar Oooh! It's useless trying to talk to you. You don't even know the difference between chalk and cheese, do you?

Hector No—but the mice never eat *my* sandwiches. (*He chortles*) Anyway, I might not be good with numbers, but I know more about science than you do.

Caspar Don't make me laugh. I know everything there *is* to know about science.

Hector Oh, yes? Well, name me a liquid that won't freeze, then.

Caspar Easy. Easy. Hot water. (*Remembering*) And talking of hot water— we're going to be right up to the neck in it if somebody finds that will before *we* do. Now come on, back up to the Mill.

Hector (*glancing off* UL) Look out. Somebody's coming.

Caspar (*looking*) It's Peter and that flea-bitten old moggy. We don't want *him* to see us here. He might ask us for money. Quick, let's nip down that sidestreet.

Hector and Caspar exit DL *as:*

Peter enters over the bridge, his few possessions in a bag tied to a stick which he carries over his shoulder. He is a handsome young man in patched, but clean clothing, and has a dejected look on his face

Puss, the cat, enters, following. He is rather old and obviously tired

Peter Come along, Puss. There's a long way to go before nightfall. (*Moving* DC) Just think, only a few days ago everything was fine, but now we've no home, no money, and nothing to eat but a crust of bread and a piece of mouldy cheese. I can understand my brothers wanting to see the back of *me*—we never did get on very well—but at least they could have let *you* stay. (*He puts down his stick and kneels beside Puss*) You've been the best cat anyone could have wished for. (*He cuddles him*) But never mind. I'll take care of you. I'm not afraid of hard work and somehow we'll manage, won't we?

Puss Miaow (*He rubs himself against Peter*)

Peter (*standing again and looking around*) Dear old Arcadia. How strange to think we may never see it again. And how I'm going to miss all my friends.

Jack and Marjory enter

Marjory (*hurrying to him*) Peter, you're not leaving yet, are you? You can't. Jack's asked the Queen *herself* to help you.

Jack Yes, she may be here at any minute.

Peter (*shaking his head*) That's very kind of you, but there wasn't any need. Really. As a matter of fact, I always wanted to see the world and this gives me a chance to do it.

Marjory (*bitterly*) But it's so unfair. Those nasty brothers of yours don't deserve a penny.

Jack And where will you go?

Peter Who knows? Dick Whittington found *his* fortune in London, but I'm afraid my cat is a little too old for killing rats. Perhaps we'll go to the New World. They say there's lots of opportunities there for a lad like me.

Marjory (*dismayed*) America? But that's *hundreds* of miles away. We'll never see you again.

Peter Don't be too sure. As soon as I'm rich and famous, we'll return to Arcadia as fast as we can. But just for now—I'm afraid there's nothing else to do except say goodbye to everyone and be on our way. (*To Puss*) Come on, Puss. Our great adventure's about to begin. We're off to *New York*.

Song 3 (Peter)

As Peter sings:

The Chorus enters and together with Jack and Marjory, join him in the song

Peter and Puss exit DR, *leaving Peter's stick behind*

The others sadly wave them off

Jack (*to Marjory; dejectedly*) I'd better go tell the Queen it's too late.
Marjory (*sighing*) I suppose so. And *we'd* better get ready for the Mid-Summer Fayre this afternoon. Though it's not going to be at all the same without Peter being there.

Everyone exits miserably as:

The Lights dim

Gruesome, the ogre's henchman, enters over the bridge. He is a sinister individual with a permanent scowl on his face, and carries a coiled whip in his hand

Gruesome (*glancing around*) So *this* is Arcadia. The perfect place to find slaves for my mighty master, Crunchbones the Ogre. (*He laughs harshly*) Now let me see . . . Where shall I look first? (*He peers into the audience*) There must be one or two *snivelling little children* out there. Perhaps I'd better climb down and have a look. (*He moves* L)

Queen Fanny enters UR. *Dressed in an outrageous costume topped by a glittering crown, she sweeps majestically* DS, *enthusiastically blowing kisses to all and sundry*

Queen (*brightly*) Hallo, darlings. Hallo. Nice to see you. No—don't stand up. It's only me. Arcadia's favourite pin-up. Your own Queen Fanny the Fifth. (*She curtsies and there is the sound of ripping*) Oops . . . I think I've just let the New Year in. (*Noticing Gruesome*) Good Heavens it's—(*well known unpopular personality*).
Gruesome (*snarling*) Silence, you old faggot. Don't you realize who I am?
Queen No. I don't. Surprise me.
Gruesome (*proudly*) I am *Gruesome*.
Queen (*eyeing him*) Gruesome? You're positively ghastly.
Gruesome Bah, Gruesome is my *name*. Henchman to the wickedest, most evil being on Earth.
Queen Oh, that's nice, dear. And how is—(*names well known politican*) these days?
Gruesome Fool. Dolt. Idiot. My master is none other than Crunchbones the Ogre. (*Pause*) King of all Ogres.
Queen (*impressed*) Oh, you don't say. Well, I'm Fanny the Fifth—Queen of Arcadia—and *Playboy*'s Playmate of the Month for January. (*She simpers*)
Gruesome (*incredulously*) "Playmate of the Month"? You?
Queen That's right, dear. (*She preens herself*)

Gruesome (*sneeringly*) I've seen better looking bodies on stockracing cars.

The Queen reacts

Queen (*to the audience; grimly*) I see. It's going to be one of *those* mornings, is it? (*To Gruesome*) Listen, Fishface, for your information every soldier in the Royal Army carries my photograph next to his heart when he goes into battle. (*She smirks*)

Gruesome (*snarling*) I'm not surprised. If your face can stop a clock, they're probably hoping it'll stop a bullet, too.

Queen Oooh. How dare you? How very dare you? Leave my kingdom at once. (*She indicates the bridge*)

Gruesome *Your* kingdom? (*He roars with laughter and cracks his whip*) You hapless old harridan. From henceforth, Crunchbones the Ogre rules Arcadia and everyone here belongs to *him*. Now out of my way. I want a closer look at this revolting little place before I begin the task of selecting suitable victims for my master's dinner table. (*He laughs harshly*)

Gruesome crosses in front of the Queen and exits DL

Queen (*to the audience*) Oh, I say, what a nasty man. He reminds me of a toothache I once had. I bet when he was little, he used to lean over the farmer's fence and shout "Mint Sauce" at the sheep. Still—if he thinks he's going to come here throwing his weight about, he's got another think coming. Because *nothing* scares me, you know. No matter how horrible it is. (*Proudly*) I've even sat through a—(*well known pop singer*) concert. No, if he shows his ugly face round here again, I'll have a word with the boys and girls and they can throw him in the nearest duck pond. (*She beams*) Now—where was I? (*Remembering*) Oh yes, I was just going to say how *nice* it is to see you all here and invite you to——

Chamberlain (*off* UL; *calling*) Your Majesty ... Your Majesty.

Queen Good Heavens, it's the Lord Chamberlain. What on earth's *he* doing here?

The Lord Chamberlain enters. He is a fussy little man, carrying his rod of office and a rolled scroll

Chamberlain (*seeing her*) Oh, Your Majesty. Thank goodness I've found you. I've been looking *everywhere*. (*He moves down to her*) You forgot your list of engagements for today. (*He holds out the scroll*)

Queen (*taking it from him*) Dear old Chamberpo—lain. I don't know what I'd do without you. (*Opening it*) Now what's this say? (*Reading*) Lunch with Mayor of—(*local Town*). Hmm. That'll be beans on toast at—(*well known "Greasy Spoon" cafe*) again. Open the Royal Flower Show. (*To the audience*) Oh, I *do* love the Flower Show. I get to give out all the prizes, you know. It's ever so exciting. I remember last year, *one* of the competitors crossed a small morse code transmitter with a huge senna pod.

Chamberlain (*surprised*) Really? And what did he get?

Queen A dot-dot-dot—and a very quick dash. (*She chortles then goes on* *reading*) Visit the Mid-Summer Fayre. Oh yes, we can't miss that, can we? There's bound to be a circus, and I *love* watching the lion tamers.

Chamberlain Really, Your Majesty?

Queen Oh, yes. They're ever so daring, you know. I remember once, I was standing next to the lion's cage when the tamer came along to do his rehearsal—and without batting an eye, he unfastened the door and went straight inside it. Well—I couldn't believe my eyes. There he was—in the middle of the lion's cage—wearing nothing but his tights and a splash of after shave, and in front of him was the biggest, most bad-tempered lion I'd ever seen in my life.

Chamberlain Good gracious.

Queen Well—it took *one* look at him, let out a roar that could have shattered a concrete mixer, and charged towards him with its mouth open and its teeth showing. Oooh. I nearly had a conniption.

Chamberlain (*fearfully*) And what happened?

Queen He dropped to his knees—stuck out his chest and showed it his muscles—and believe this or believe it not, that lion stopped dead in its tracks, lay down on the floor and started to lick him all over. (*She makes licking noises*) Oh it was absolutely *amazing*. Then after a few minutes, the lion tamer looked up at me and said, "How about that, then, Missis Queen? I bet *you* couldn't do that, could you?" I said, "You get that lion out of there, and I'll show you."

Chamberlain (*changing the subject*) Well—that's all very interesting, Your Majesty, but we *really* ought to be getting along. The Prime Minister wishes to see you rather urgently, I'm afraid. There's been another all night sitting in the House of Commons.

Queen Oh dear, and I've warned them *dozens* of times about that lamb curry. (*Briskly*) Very well, Chamberlain—whisk me back to the Palace. I'll speak to those crooks at the Mill this afternoon. (*To the audience*) You will excuse me, won't you? Duty calls, I'm afraid. See you all later. Bye-bye, everyone. Bye-bye.

The Queen and the Chamberlain exit DR *as:*

Freckles, the page, enters cautiously UR. *He is a zany character wearing over-large Royal livery and has a ready smile. He scuttles down* C, *looks from side to side, then hurries back* UR *and signals off*

Freckles (*calling softly*) It's all right, Princess. They've gone.

Princess Miranda enters UR. *She is a very attractive girl in a simple gown, with a warm and friendly personality*

They move down C

Princess (*laughing*) Oh, Freckles, thank goodness you saw them in time. Mother would be furious if she knew I'd sneaked out of the Palace without telling anyone—and especially dressed like this.

Freckles I know. And she wouldn't be all that pleased with *me*, either. I'm supposed to be looking after you, you know—not letting you go wandering round the countryside in disguise.

Princess But I've never been to this part of Arcadia before, and it's so nice not to be recognized. (*Looking around*) Oh isn't this beautiful? It must be the prettiest village in the whole kingdom. Look at these lovely little shops and houses.

Freckles Don't mention shops to me. I had to go shopping with your mother, yesterday and she spent six hours in—(*local department store*).

Princess Six hours? What on earth did she buy?

Freckles Nothing. She got stuck in the lift. (*He chortles*)

Princess (*amused*) I don't believe a *word* of it, Freckles. You know as well as I do that mother never uses the lifts.

Freckles She didn't have much choice, did she? I mean, she couldn't go up on the escalator.

Princess Why not?

Freckles There was a notice at the side of it that said, "Dogs must be carried"—and we didn't have a dog with us.

Princess (*giggling*) Oh, Freckles. You *do* make me laugh. It's going to be lovely having you for a stepfather.

Freckles Oh, I don't know about that, Princess. I don't think your mother fancies me any more. She said I embarrassed her at the banquet last night.

Princess Why? What on earth did you do?

Freckles I drank eight glasses of Coca Cola—and burped Seven-Up. (*He sees Peter's stick and bundle*) Hallo—what's this? (*He picks it up*) Somebody must have dropped it.

Princess (*concerned*) Oh, dear. You'd better take it to the Police Station. I'm sure the owner will be looking for it.

Freckles (*scornfully*) No, it probably belongs to some old tramp. (*He looks inside the bundle*) There's nothing in it except a shirt and some bread and cheese.

Princess All the same, it could be everything the poor man owns. Please, Freckles.

Freckles (*cheerfully*) All right, then. You wait here and I'll be back in a minute. Don't talk to any strange men.

Freckles exits DR

The Princess watches him go, then moves DC *gazing at the buildings with interest*

Gruesome enters UR, *gazing back over his trail*

Gruesome (*gloatingly*) What a snug little haven of unsuspecting victims. (*He gives an evil chuckle*) And how fortunate I happened to stumble upon it. My master, the Ogre, will be well pleased with my discovery. (*He turns and notices the Princess*) What's this? (*Awed*) By the eye-teeth of Crunchbones himself—the most beautiful female I've ever seen. If I return to his castle with *her*, who knows how great my reward will be? (*Loudly*) Ahem. (*He moves down towards her*)

Princess (*turning and seeing him*) Oh—(*nervously*) good-morning.

Gruesome (*leering*) All the better for seeing *you*, my pretty one. You'll make a tasty little morsel for my master's dinner. (*He grabs her wrist*)

Princess (*startled*) What? (*Struggling*) Let go of me. Let go.
Gruesome (*laughing*) To the Ogre's castle. (*He attempts to drag her away*)
Princess (*calling*) Help! Help! (*She beats at him*)

Gruesome and the Princess continue to struggle as:

Peter enters DR

Peter (*seeing the struggle*) What? (*He hurries over and grabs Gruesome*)
Hands off, you ugly brute. Take that. (*He hits him*)

Gruesome howls and falls

Peter turns to the Princess

> *Gruesome scrambles to his feet again and exits, hurrying off over the bridge*

Are you all right, Miss?
Princess (*recovering herself*) Yes, thank you. But I don't know *what* I'd
have done if you hadn't come along. You must tell me your name at once
and I'll see that you're richly rewarded.
Peter (*embarrassed*) Oh, there's no need for that. I'm only too pleased to
have been of service.
Princess But I'd still like to know who you are. It isn't every day I'm rescued
by a handsome young man.
Peter (*laughing*) I don't know about handsome, but my name is Peter—
youngest son of the village's late Miller.
Princess (*interested*) Then you live in the Mill house, do you?
Peter Not any more, I'm afraid. I was turned out of it this very morning
and was just leaving here to seek my fortune, when I realized I'd already
lost the few possessions I had. They were tied in a bundle to the end of an
old stick. That's what I was looking for when I heard your shouts.
Princess (*with her eyes sparkling*) Then perhaps *I* can help you find your
possessions *and* your fortune.
Peter (*puzzled*) You can? But how?
Princess (*eagerly*) Promise that you won't leave the village until I return.
Peter (*still puzzled*) If you insist—but I don't understand.
Princess Don't worry, just meet me at the Fayre this afternoon and I think
you'll be in for a *big* surprise.

The Princess exits UR *as:*

Puss enters DR

Peter (*calling after her*) Wait—you still haven't . . . Too late. She's gone. (*To
Puss*) Oh, Puss—I've just met the most beautiful girl I've ever seen in my
life—and I don't even know her name. (*He frowns*) But whatever did she
mean by saying she could help me make my fortune? Well—I suppose I'll
just have to wait and see. (*To Puss*) Come on, old friend. We may as well
take a walk until it's time for the Fayre to begin.

Peter and Puss exit DR *as:*

Gruesome enters over the bridge. He watches them go

Gruesome (*snarling*) You'll pay for this, Master Peter. No-one lays a finger
on Gruesome and gets away with it. Then once I've dealt with *you*, the girl
will be *mine*—and my master, the Ogre shall dine on her for supper. (*He
roars with evil laughter*)

Gruesome exits as:

Mother Goose enters DR, *smiling cheerfully*

Mother Goose Oh no, cruel Master Gruesome, you'll find your plan's no
use.
No harm shall come to anyone, as sure as my name's
Mother Goose.
Despite old Crunchbones' magic powers, I rather fancy that
Your downfall will be hastened by young Peter's old and
faithful cat.
I'll change his image—yet, of course, retain his feline
roots . . .
And "poor old Puss" shall be re-born as talking, walking
Puss in Boots.

Black-out

SCENE 2

*A quiet street with a backdrop depicting cottages and trees. A sunny day. A
lane scene*

Caspar and Hector enter L

Caspar (*annoyed*) I don't believe it. I don't *believe* it. We've been all the way
home and back again, and *still* we haven't found that will. This is all *your*
fault, you know. You're the one to blame.
Hector Oh, yes, go on, blame me. I get the blame for everything, I do. The
way *you* go on, anybody would think I was stupid.
Caspar You *are* stupid, stupid. Look at the time you crashed the car and the
policeman asked what gear you were in when it happened. What did you
tell him? (*Mockingly*) A black and white striped shirt, Bermuda shorts
and a pink woolly hat with a pom-pom on it.
Hector (*embarrassed*) Well—anybody can make a mistake. And anyway—
At least I'm not as daft as *you* are. *I* don't go round telling folks there's a
talking plant growing in our back garden.
Caspar But there *is*. I bought it at—(*names local garden centre*) and it's never
stopped talking since I planted it. The only trouble is, I don't know what
kind of plant it is. There wasn't any label on it, you see.
Hector Well, what sort of things does it say?
Caspar It says—er—"Thank you for letting me live in your lovely garden.
This must be the best garden in—(*own district*), "It's a real privilege to be
planted here" and "I bet nobody else in the whole wide world knows as
much about growing things as *you* do."

Hector (*realizing*) Oooh. *I* know what kind of plant *that* is.
Caspar (*eagerly*) What? What?
Hector It's a *creeper.*
Caspar (*pushing him violently*) Idiot. Come here and listen. What are we going to do about the will? If the wrong person finds it, we're done for.

Gruesome enters L, *holding the will*

Gruesome (*with a sneering laugh*) Could *this* be what you're looking for? (*He displays the will*) I found it on the footpath outside the village.
Hector ⎱ (*together*) Oo-er. (*They retreat from him*)
Caspar ⎰
Gruesome (*advancing*) So—you were going to cheat your brother out of his inheritance, were you? (*He glowers at them*)
Caspar (*trembling*) Oh, don't give us away, Mister.
Hector They'll put us in the stocks and throw loads of rubbish at us.
Gruesome (*thoughtfully*) Indeed? Then suppose I were to keep this our little secret—in exchange for your help in a certain matter? What then?
Caspar (*eagerly*) Oh, yes. We'll do anything—(*to Hector*) won't we, Hector?
Hector (*nodding rapidly*) Anything at all.
Gruesome (*smirking*) Yes, I thought you might. (*He tucks the will into his belt*) Very well, then. Tell me this. Which one of you is the *bravest?*
Caspar Eh? (*Quickly*) Oh, that's *me.* Me. I used to be a bank guard once, and one day this real nasty crook came in and tried to rob it. So quick as a flash, I pulled out my gun—(*miming it*), looked him straight in the eye, and told him if he took one more step I'd let him have it.
Gruesome And what happened?
Caspar He *took* one more step, so I *did* let him have it. (*Easily*) Well—I never wanted the stupid old gun, anyway.
Gruesome Bah. What I'm looking for is someone *responsible.*
Hector Oh, well—in that case, you needn't look any further, need you? *I'm* here. (*He smirks and poses*)
Gruesome (*eyeing him in disbelief*) You?
Hector Yes. Every time something goes wrong round here, folk say I'm responsible.
Gruesome (*annoyed*) Aghhhh. Enough of this stupidity. Follow me and I'll tell you exactly what it is I want you to do.

Gruesome turns and exits L, *followed by Caspar and Hector as:*

Freckles enters R

Freckles (*calling*) Princess? Princess? (*To the audience*) Here—you haven't seen the Princess anywhere, have you? I only left her for a few minutes and now she's vanished. (*Worriedly*) Oh, if her mother finds out she's missing, she'll go *crackers.* Mind you—that shouldn't take her long. She's half crackers already. (*Realizing*) Here—but I shouldn't make fun, should I? I mean—she's not on her own. There's lots of funny folk around these days. (*Confidentially*) I read in the—(*local paper*) the other day, that *one* person out of every *four* is a bit peculiar. *One* out of *four.* It's a bit worrying, isn't it? So when you get home tonight, check your friends—

and if three of them seem to be all right, then the fourth one's got to be you. (*He chortles, then changes the subject*) Anyway—I can't stand here all morning talking to you, can I? I've got to find the Princess. (*Glancing off* L) Oooh, *here's* somebody who might have seen her, it's the little village children.

The Babes enter, looking downcast

(*Brightly*) Hiya kids, I was just looking for the Princess and I—(*Noticing*) Hey—hey—What's the matter? Why so sad?

Babe 1 It's the Mid-Summer Fayre this afternoon, and everyone's dressing up for it.

Babe 2 But *our* mummies and daddies are too poor to buy *new* clothes . . .

Babe 3 So the Queen won't even notice *us*.

The Babes all agree sadly

Freckles (*solemnly*) I *see*. (*Thinking*) Well, *I* know the Queen as well as anybody, and I can tell *you*, that the thing she likes to see best of all is a nice big *smile*—so if you all wear big smiles, she's bound to notice you, isn't she? (*He beams at them*)

Babe 4 (*doubtfully*) Even though we haven't got new clothes on?

Freckles (*nodding*) Even though you haven't got new clothes on. After all— it's like she says herself—rich or poor, it doesn't matter *what* you're wearing as long as you remember to crown it all with a smile.

Song 4 (Freckles and children)

The Babes dance off with Freckles at the end of the song

Rapid fade to Black-out

SCENE 3

The Mid-Summer Fayre

A Fairground with a backdrop depicting usual funfair attractions, a circus tent, slides, roundabouts, etc., with glimpses of wooded hills behind. R *is a fortune-teller's tent, or caravan, with a practical opening, and* L *are stalls and trees*

When the scene begins, gypsies are performing a spirited Hora to a cheering crowd of Villagers. This should be as bright and fast moving as possible

Dance (Gypsies)

As the dance ends, there is much applause from the crowd

The Lord Chamberlain enters up L, *carrying his rod of office which he bangs on the ground to gain attention*

Chamberlain (*grandly*) Her Royal Majesty, Queen Fanny the Fifth of Arcadia.

The Chorus cheer loudly as:

The Queen enters DL *and moves down* C *with the Chamberlain following*

Queen (*to the crowd; graciously*) Thank you. Thank you. (*To the audience*) Oh, I say—I *am* enjoying meself this afternoon. Every time I've had a ride on something, folk gave me things to eat and drink. Hot dogs, toffee apples, candy floss, brandy snap, ice cream, sticks of rock, baked potatoes, Coca Cola, orange squash, milk shakes. Oooh. I think I gained *ten kilos* on the swings alone. (*She chuckles and smooths her hips*) Mind you—like they always say—What you gain on the swings, you'll lose on the roundabouts—and I *did* . . . (*She burps and dabs at her mouth genteely*) But I love funfairs, don't you, boys and girls?

Audience reaction

Yes, of course you do. You can meet all your friends there, can't you? I met one feller here this afternoon who used to be a *magician*. Yes, he came to the Palace once and sawed his pretty young girl assistant in half. Ever so clever, he was. Of course, she's given up showbusiness now. She's living in Leeds and Birmingham.

Chamberlain (*clearing his throat*) Ahem. (*He indicates the Chorus*)

Queen (*contrite*) Oh, I *am* sorry. I'm at it again, aren't I? Gossiping away when I should be attending to me Royal duties.(*To the Chorus*) Won't keep you a moment, dears. Just waiting for me daughter. (*To the Chamberlain*) Where's she got to, Chamberlain? We can't start the Parade without *her*.

The Princess hurries on DR. *She is now wearing a beautiful gown and tiara*

Princess Here I am, Mother. Sorry I'm late.

The Chorus bow and curtsy

Queen (*annoyed*) I should think so too, dear. Where on earth have you been?

Princess Oh, Mother, I've had the most awful experience.

Queen (*accusingly*) You've not been watching—(*TV Soap*) again, have you?

Princess No, no, this was *far* worse than that. Some dreadful man tried to kidnap me.

Queen (*aghast*) Aaaaagh. (*Dramatically*) History repeats itself.

Princess (*surprised*) Whatever do you mean, Mother?

Queen I was kidnapped meself, once—by a gang of bloodthirsty Irishmen. Oooh, they were nasty. They threatened to chop me into tiny little pieces if your father didn't give them the Crown Jewels.

Princess But we've still got the Crown Jewels, Mother, so how did you escape?

Queen They sent me back to the Palace with the ransom note. (*She chortles*) Anyway—never mind about that. You should have been here ages ago. Everybody's waiting for us to start the Parade.

Princess Yes, I know, Mother, but there's something I've got to *tell* you. Something *wonderful*.

Queen (*waving it aside*) You'll have to do it later, dear. They're tuning up the instruments already. Can't you hear them?

Vamp begins under dialogue

Princess But it's important, Mother. *Very* important.

Queen And so's getting this Parade off. (*Ecstatically*) Oh, the drums—the trumpets—the combs and paper. (*Loudly*) On with the Parade. (*She waves her arms wildly*)

Song 5 (Queen and Chorus)

At the end of the song, the Queen triumphantly takes the Princess and the Chamberlain by the arms and leads everyone off, singing a reprise which fades into the distance

Peter and Puss enter DL *when the stage is empty*

Peter (*wearily*) Well, we've been here for ages, but I haven't seen a sign of her, yet. How about you, Puss?

Puss (*shaking his head*) Miaow.

Peter We *could* have missed her in the crowd, I suppose. Everyone in the world seems to be here this afternoon. Perhaps we'd better go back the way we came and look again?

Puss (*tiredly*) Miaow. (*He lies down and closes his eyes*)

Peter (*concerned*) Poor old Puss. You have walked a long way today, haven't you? No wonder you're tired. (*He smiles*) I'll tell you what. You stay here and rest while *I* go back. And don't worry. It shouldn't take me more than twenty minutes. See you later.

Peter exits UL *as:*

Mother Goose appears DR. *She carries a pair of red boots*

Mother Goose (*smiling*) And now it's time to play *my* part . . .
        For here's the special charm
        That's needed to enable Puss
        To keep his master free from harm. (*She displays the boots*)
        With magic boots upon his paws,
        And a twinkle in his eyes,
        He'll prove a match for all his foes . . .
        As very soon they'll realize.
        So waken from your dreams, friend cat . . . (*She points at the sleeping cat with her wooden spoon and twirls it*)

There is a tinkling of triangles

Puss wakes

        There's duty to be done.
        Come, follow me . . . And with *your* help
        Young Peter's fortune *shall* be won.

With a flourish of her spoon, Mother Goose exits into the fortune-teller's tent (or caravan) followed by Puss. As they vanish from sight:

Marjory Daw enters from behind it, with a reluctant Jack Spratt behind her

Marjory (*urgently*) Hurry, Jack. Hurry. (*She pulls him* CF)
Jack (*protesting*) But we're missing the Parade.
Marjory Never mind the silly old Parade. This is *much* more important. I thought I saw Peter a few moments ago. Standing right here.
Jack (*surprised*) Peter? But you couldn't have done. He'll be miles away by now.
Marjory Maybe he's changed his mind and come back again? (*Glancing around*) Oh, I'm *sure* it was him.

Freckles enters DL. *He is carrying Peter's stick and bundle on his shoulder*

Freckles (*to the audience*) Hiya, kids. (*He waves at them*)
Marjory (*surprised*) Look. (*She points at the stick*)
Jack (*surprised*) Peter's stick and belongings.

Jack and Marjory hurry over to Freckles

Jack taps him on the shoulder

(*Grimly*) Excuse me—those things you're carrying. Do you mind telling me where you got them from?
Freckles Oh—are they yours?
Jack No, they're not. But they *do* belong to a friend of ours and we'd like to know what they're doing in *your* possession.
Freckles Oh ... Well ... We found them in the Village Square this morning—me and the Princess——
Marjory (*interrupting*) Princess?
Freckles That's right. Princess Miranda. (*Proudly*) I'm Freckles, the Queen's Page. (*He beams at them*)
Jack (*horrified*) Oh, my goodness. And we almost accused you of stealing.
Marjory We thought you were a thief.
Freckles (*indignantly*) Well I'll be pasteurized.
Jack (*contrite*) We're awfully sorry—but you must admit it looked suspicious. A total stranger walking around the fairground with Peter's possessions.
Freckles (*grudgingly*) Well—I suppose it did. But you shouldn't go jumping to confusions, you know. I've only brought 'em here so the Princess can give 'em back to him.
Marjory (*puzzled*) But how did she know they were *his*?
Freckles Because he *told* her they were, didn't he? That's why she's meeting him here this afternoon. To thank him for saving her life.
Jack (*surprised*) What?
Freckles Oh, yes. This nasty looking feller was collecting dinners for some Ogre or other, and tried to take *her*. If it hadn't been for your friend, we'd never have seen her again.
Marjory How awful. (*Brightening*) But if Peter *did* rescue the Princess, the Queen's *bound* to help him claim his share of the Mill, isn't she? (*To Jack*) Oh Jack, everything's turning out right, after all.

Jack It certainly seems like it. (*Relieved*) And that means there'll be no need for him to leave Arcadia. Come on. Let's find the others and break the good news. (*To Freckles*) Bye.

Jack and Marjory exit happily UR

Freckles (*to the audience; fondly*) What a lovely couple. It must be real nice having friends like that. Mind you—even your *best* friends can be a bit peculiar sometimes, can't they? I mean—take Queen Fanny for instance. She was reading a book yesterday. All about Cleopatra, the Temptress of the Nile. Do you know why Cleopatra was so beautiful? Well it told you in the book. She used to bathe herself in milk every bath-night. Litres and litres of milk. Well, of course, if it was good enough for Cleopatra, it was good enough for Fanny, so off she went down to—(*a local dairy*) and ordered an extra five hundred bottles. "Do you want it pasteurized?" the milkman asked her. "Oh, no" she said, "Up to me knees'll be fine".

The Princess enters UR, *looking anxious*

Princess (*seeing him*) Freckles. (*She hurries down to him*) Thank goodness you're here. Have you seen him?
Freckles (*shaking his head*) No. Not a sign.
Princess (*concerned*) But he promised he'd be here. He *promised*.
Freckles (*cheerfully*) Don't worry, Princess. There's hours before the Fayre closes.
Princess But I want to introduce him to Mother before she leaves for the Flower Show.
Freckles Oh, you've told her about him, have you?
Princess (*ruefully*) I haven't had the chance. But I just *know* she's going to love him as much as *I* do. I *know* it.
Freckles (*startled*) *Love* him? But you've only just *met* him.
Princess (*dreamily*) I know. And he's the handsomest man in all Arcadia. (*Eagerly*) Oh, Freckles. I can't wait to see him again.
Freckles Blimey. You *have* got it bad, haven't you?
Princess (*laughing*) Oh, *yes*. I think so.

Song 6 (Princess)

At the end of the song, the Princess and Freckles exit DR *as:*

Peter enters UL

Peter (*miserably*) Not a sign of her, and I've been all around the Fairground. Come on, Puss. It looks as though we're wasting our time. (*He notices Puss is missing*) Puss? (*Looking around*) Puss? (*Alarmed*) Where are you?

Mother Goose enters from the tent

(*To her; anxiously*) Excuse me. But you haven't seen a cat, have you? He's rather old and toothless, but he's all I have left in the world.

Mother Goose That aged cat you claim as a friend.
                      Has gone from you forever.

Peter reacts in dismay

                      He's been transformed by magic power . . .
                      Is younger now . . . and *far* more clever.
                      Place your trust in his advice
                      And let him be your guide,
                      For if you do, you'll find you're led
                      To fame and fortune . . . and a bride.

   Mother Goose exits R, *quickly*

Peter (*startled*) What? (*Realizing she is gone*) Wait. (*He hurries* R) Too late.
She's gone. (*Puzzled*) What on earth could she have meant? It didn't
make the slightest bit of sense to me.

   Puss cartwheels onto the stage from the tent (or springs from the caravan).
   He is now slim and lithe in leotard, tights, the red boots and a cat-mask

Puss But it did to *me*.
Peter (*astounded*) Who are you?
Puss (*in rap tempo with movement*) I'm a real cool cat
                      With brains for two,
                      So stick with me, kid,
                      Whatever you do:
                      And if fame and fortune is what you seek,
                      Then I'll see that you get them both within the week.
                      For all your worries, don't you give two hoots,
                      'Cos I'm gonna solve them—I'm Puss in Boots. *Yeah.* (*He
                          strikes an attitude*)
Peter (*astounded*) I don't believe it. A talking *cat*.
Puss And what's wrong with that, might I ask?
Peter Why—nothing at all. It's just that I've never heard a cat speak before.
Puss (*airily*) Oh, you'd be surprised what cats can do when they put their
mind to it. We're much cleverer than humans, you know.
Peter Really?
Puss Of course. Take *me*, for instance. *I* know everything there is to know
about sport. (*He breathes on his claws and polishes them on his chest*)
Peter Sport?
Puss Yes. Ask me a question, and I'll prove it to you.
Peter (*amused*) All right. (*Thinking*) Let's say you're playing football and
somebody scores—what do you get?
Puss (*airily*) Easy—a goal.
Peter And in cricket?
Puss A run.
Peter Then what do you get in bowls?
Puss Goldfish.

Peter laughs

(*Indignantly*) What's so funny?

Peter (*sobering*) I'm terribly sorry. You're absolutely right, of course.

Puss Naturally. I always *am*. And that's why you've got to do exactly as I say if we're going to make your fortune. Now then—the first thing we need is a nice fat rabbit.

Peter (*surprised*) A rabbit?

Puss That's right. There's nothing like a rabbit for making fortunes. So where's the best place to find one?

Peter Why—in the fields outside the village, I suppose. But . . .

Puss (*briskly*) No time for explanations. There's work to be done and not much time to do it in. Come on, Master Peter. From now on, we're partners—and no-one's going to separate us until I've made you the happiest man in Arcadia.

Song 7 (Puss and Peter)

If required, the Chorus may enter and join in the song

At the end of the song, Puss and Peter exit

Black-out

SCENE 4

Outside the Palace

A lane scene depicting the exterior of a Palace and grounds. If this is not possible, the scene can be played in front of a plain lane cloth

Caspar and Hector enter L. They are both looking worried

Hector (*shaking his head*) I don't like it. I don't like it. It's not right.

Caspar (*irritated*) Will you stop *saying* that. I know you don't like it. *I* don't like it, either, but if we don't do as he tells us, we're going to be in *real* trouble.

Hector Yes, but kidnapping people for an Ogre's dinner isn't very nice, is it? I mean—some of them might be friends of ours.

Caspar What do you mean, some of them might be friends of ours? We haven't *got* any friends. That's why we got rid of Peter, isn't it? Because he was popular and we weren't.

Hector (*with his face crumpling*) I know. It's terrible not to have any friends.

Caspar (*sourly*) Huh, who cares about friends, anyway? We've still got each other.

Hector (*brightening*) Yes, you're right. And if you died before me, I'd go to your grave every week and leave little presents on top of it, just to show how much I missed you.

Caspar (*touched*) Would you really, Hector? That's the nicest thing you've ever said to me. (*Pause*) Er—what sort of presents would you bring?

Hector Oh—boxes and boxes of your favourite cigars.

Caspar Cor, smashing. And what about the matches to light 'em with?

Hector (*shaking his head*) No, you wouldn't need matches where you're going.

As Caspar reacts and pushes Hector:

Gruesome enters

Gruesome (*snarling*) So, this is where you're hiding yourselves, eh? (*He moves towards them*) Well—have you done it?

Caspar (*protesting*) Give over. We've hardly had time to look round.

Gruesome (*annoyed*) Time? It's over two hours since I saw you last, and my Master the Ogre grows hungrier by the minute.

Hector (*helpfully*) Couldn't you buy him a Big Mac to be going on with?

Gruesome (*snarling*) Bah. I'll give you one more chance to find suitable victims, and if you *fail* me . . . (*He pats the will in his belt*)

Caspar (*quickly*) Don't worry, Mr Gruesome. We won't let you down.

Hector We'll have 'em queuing up to get eaten. Honest we will.

Gruesome Good. Now get on with it. (*Loudly*) Move.

Caspar and Hector quickly exit R

(*Sourly*) Bungling fools. They'll be the *first* to roast in my master's oven. But now to resume my own search and find that beautiful girl I saw earlier.

Queen Fanny enters L

Queen (*coyly*) Looking for me? (*Recognizing him*) Oh, no, it's him again. The original Nightmare on Elm Street.

Gruesome So—(*moving towards her*) you remember me, do you?

Queen Well—I've forgotten the name, but the *breath's* familiar. (*She grimaces and wafts it away*)

Gruesome Bah, out of my way, you wizened old hag.

Queen Wizened? *Wizened*? (*She simpers*) Don't be ridiculous. Only last month, *Woman's Own* said I looked as beautiful as a seventeen year old and had a skin like a peach.

Gruesome Have you ever *seen* a seventeen year old peach?

Queen (*after a reaction*) Oh, come on. There's no need to be so nasty. Life's too short. I mean—why don't you relax a bit? Have a laugh—look in a mirror.

Gruesome (*snarling*) Don't talk to me about mirrors. I *hate* mirrors.

Queen (*aside*) I'm not surprised. (*To him*) Oh, you don't mean that. Not *really*. What's wrong with mirrors?

Gruesome Break a mirror, and you have seven years' bad luck.

Queen (*amused*) Don't be silly. Of course you don't. My brother broke a mirror once, and *he* didn't have seven years' bad luck.

Gruesome Didn't he?

Queen No, he got run over by a steamroller the same afternoon.

The Princess enters R, *distractedly*

Princess Mother. I—(*seeing Gruesome*) Oh. It's him. The man who tried to kidnap me. (*She recoils*)

Queen (*startled*) Eh? Oooh. Quick. Call out the guards.

The Princess turns to flee

Gruesome (*leaping forward*) Not so fast, pretty one. (*He grabs her*) You're coming with me.
Princess (*struggling*) Help. Help.
Queen (*in a panic*) Help.

> *Puss enters. He carries a small sack over his shoulder and carries a small dagger in his belt*

Puss Oho. (*Dropping the sack, he hurries over to Gruesome and taps him on the shoulder*) Excuse me.

Gruesome releases the Princess and turns to him

Knock, knock.
Gruesome (*puzzled*) Who's there?
Puss Broker.
Gruesome (*snarling*) Broker who?
Puss Broker few toes for you.

Puss stamps hard on Gruesome's foot

Gruesome howls with pain, clutches his foot and dances around on one leg

Puss pulls out his dagger and jabs him mercilessly

> *Shrieking in pain, Gruesome hops off* R, *and exits*

(*Laughing*) That's got rid of *him*.
Queen (*gaping*) Blimey. It's Garfield.
Puss (*bowing deeply*) Your Majesty. (*To the Princess*) Highness. Allow me to introduce myself. Puss in Boots, Squire to that great and noble young gentleman, the Marquis of Carabosse.
Princess But—but you're a *cat*.
Puss Indeed I am. And the cleverest cat in Arcadia, if I say so myself. (*He looks smug and preens himself*)
Queen Well I don't know about that, but you're certainly the *bravest*. If it hadn't been for you, I don't know *what* would have happened. Thank goodness you came along.
Puss As a matter of fact, I was just on my way to the Palace. My master, the Marquis, has been out hunting and thought you might like a nice juicy rabbit for your dinner table.
Queen Oooh, I say. Isn't that kind of him? I love rabbit.
Puss (*picking up the sack*) With the compliments of the Marquis of Carabosse. (*He hands it to her*)
Queen (*peering into the sack*) Ooh, isn't it a big one? There'll be enough here to make a rabbit pie *and* some rabbit beer.
Princess Rabbit beer? What on earth's that?
Queen Well—it's the same as ordinary beer, but it's got more hops in it. (*She chortles*) I couldn't resist that. (*She sobers*) Well now, I don't know what to say. I mean—it's a long time since anybody sent me presents.

(*Thoughtfully*) The Marquis of Carabosse, eh? I can't say I remember him. But I'll tell you what. First thing tomorrow morning we'll pay him a visit and thank him personally.

Puss (*taken aback*) Tomorrow? (*Aside*) Oh, my paws and whiskers.

Queen Where does he live? It's not *too* far, is it?

Puss (*thinking quickly*) Why—er—no. Not far at all, Your Majesty. But unfortunately my master won't be at home tomorrow. He—er—he'll be inspecting his Estates—beyond the crossroads.

Queen Oooh, I say, we've never been out that way before, have we, Miranda? I'll tell you what. We'll get the Royal coach to take us there, first thing, and maybe we can all have a picnic together. (*She beams*)

Princess (*protesting*) But I'm going back to the village tomorrow morning, Mother. To try and find Peter.

Queen Don't be silly, dear. If he'd wanted to see you again, he'd have turned up at the Fayre as he promised, wouldn't he? Besides, I've already told you—you can't *possibly* be in love with him. You've only met him the once and he's nothing but a poor *Miller*'s son. This Marquis of Carabosse sounds a *lot* more interesting. (*To Puss*) Tell your Master we'll see him in the morning. (*To the Princess*) Come along, Miranda.

The Queen exits with the sack, followed by the reluctant Princess

Puss   (*dismayed*) Here's a pretty how'd'you do.
I've landed Peter in the stew.
One Royal *visit*, I'd not planned.
He needs fine clothes, and Castle grand.
Think fast . . . (*He thinks*) Ah, yes—I have it now.
(*Smugly*) There's none so smart as me, I vow.
The answer's clear. One has to laugh . . .
Tomorrow he must have a *bath*.

Puss exits, laughing delightedly

Black-out

SCENE 5

A Clearing by the Lakeside

Full set. The backdrop depicts a country scene with cornfields, trees and perhaps a distant farm. Trees and thick shrubs mask entrances L and R, and a signpost points R to the lake and L to Arcadia

When the scene begins, girls in bright gingham dresses, and boys in check shirts and jeans are performing a lively barndance, led by Jack and Marjory. Rolled towels and picnic baskets are dotted about the clearing

Song 8 and Dance (Jack, Marjory and Chorus)

At the end of the song, the Chorus break into small groups and chat animatedly but quietly. Some take their towels and exit in the direction of the lake

Marjory (*happily*) Oh, isn't it lovely here in the countryside? It's a perfect day for a picnic.

Jack Yes, but I'd enjoy it more if we knew what had happened to Peter. No-one's seen him since yesterday morning, and he never turned up to meet the Princess.

Marjory (*anxiously*) You don't think anything's happened to him, do you?

Jack (*reassuringly*) Oh, I shouldn't think so. But it's certainly strange. As soon as we get back to the village, we'd better see if we can find him.

Marjory Good idea. (*She glances off* L) Oh.

Jack What is it?

Marjory Those horrible brothers of his are coming this way. Who invited *them* to the picnic?

Jack (*disgustedly*) Well it certainly wasn't me. (*To the others*) Come on, everybody. Down to the lake before they arrive here. We don't want to mix with *their* sort.

Jack and Marjory exit R

The Chorus quickly grab their things and follow as:

Caspar and Hector enter L

Hector (*looking around*) Here, they've all gone.

Caspar (*annoyed*) Bah, they must have seen us coming.

Hector Rotten things. How can we kidnap 'em if they keep running away? (*He calls* R) Come back. The Ogre wants you for his dinner.

Caspar (*alarmed and hitting him*) Keep your voice down, you fathead. We don't want 'em knowing who we're working for. It's supposed to be a *secret*. (*Disgusted*) Oooh, I sometimes wonder if you've got any brains at all.

Hector Eh?

Caspar Honestly, you're so *stupid*, you don't even know what you're *doing*, half the time.

Hector (*indignantly*) Yes, I do.

Caspar All right, then. All right. *Prove* it to me. Imagine you're standing in a queue at the ticket office in—(*local railway station*).

Hector (*repeating the station name*) Right. I'm standing in the queue. (*He poses*)

Caspar You're behind a fat woman with red hair and spectacles who wants to go to Bradford, and a one-legged Chinaman in a kilt who's trying to buy a ticket to Ashby-de-la-Zouch.

Hector Yes, yes.

Caspar So tell me—where are *you* going?

Hector (*startled*) Eh?

Caspar I said, where are *you* going?

Hector (*blankly*) How do *I* know where I'm going?

Caspar (*triumphantly*) You see? You've got no idea, have you? (*Heavily*) Well if you don't know where you're going, *why are you standing in the queue*? (*He pushes him*) Now listen, you heard what old Gruesome said last night? If we don't kidnap somebody soon, we're going to be in *big* trouble. This is our last chance.

Hector Huh. It's all right for him to say, but how are we going to do it? They're always in a gang, aren't they? And as soon as they see *us* coming, they clear off.

Caspar So what *we* have to do, is wait till we see one of 'em on their own and take 'em by *surprise*. Right?

Hector But we could be waiting ages.

Caspar No we couldn't. They've all to come back to the village tonight, haven't they? And if we hide by the bridge, we can grab the last one over it, take 'em straight to old Gruesome and get that will back without any trouble at all. (*He chortles*) By this time tomorrow, we won't have a thing to worry about.

Hector (*delightedly*) You're right. You're right. Quick. Let's get back and find a good hiding place.

Hector and Caspar exit L, *chuckling with glee as:*

Puss and Peter enter L

Puss Here we are. Now don't forget. Do just as I've told you, and leave the rest to me.

Peter But I haven't got a bathing suit.

Puss (*airily*) Who needs a bathing suit, *I* don't.

Peter Yes, but you're a *cat*. And anyway, you still haven't told me why it's so important for me to go swimming.

Puss (*groaning*) Oh, my paws and whiskers. (*Firmly*) Look, do you want to make your fortune and marry the Princess, or don't you?

Peter If it's all the same to you, I'd sooner marry the girl I met in the village yesterday.

Puss Then hurry up and get out of those awful clothes or you won't marry *anyone*.

Peter (*wistfully*) Do you think I *will* see her again, Puss? The girl from the village.

Puss Providing you stop asking silly questions and get into the water.

Peter I know it sounds silly, but I can't get her out of my mind. She was so *beautiful*. Like ... Like ... (*He is lost for words*)

Puss A dish of Kit-e-Kat?

Peter (*amused*) Oh Puss, I don't expect *you* to understand, but I can't imagine living my life without her. To *me* she was absolute *perfection*. The most sensational girl I've ever seen.

Song 9 (Peter)

Puss may join in this song if required

After the song, Puss grabs hold of Peter's arm and drags him R

Puss To the *lake*.

Puss and Peter exit RC *as:*

Gruesome enters

Gruesome (*angrily*) By the great eye teeth of Crunchbones, the Ogre, my patience has come to an end. Those dolts I despatched to find victims *still* haven't returned, and the Royal Palace is so heavily guarded I had no chance to sneak in and grab the Princess. (*Leering*) But my mighty master shall not go hungry. How lucky I spotted Master Peter and that mangy cat of his and managed to follow them here unseen. They'll make a tasty snack for his midday meal. (*He chuckles*)

Mother Goose enters R

Mother Goose (*cheerily*) Don't count your chicks before they hatch.
There's still a way to go
Ere Peter and his cat you catch,
As very soon you'll know.
Despite your firm intentions
They'll foil ev'rything you do ...
And ere tomorrow morning comes
Will end your life—and Crunchbones' too.

Gruesome (*sneering*) Well, well, well. If it isn't that meddlesome old hag, Mother Goose. My master warned me about *you*. I wondered how long it would be before you poked your nose into things that didn't concern you. (*He swaggers closer to her*) So, you think this pathetic pair of pipsqueaks will get the better of *me*, do you? And how will they do *that*, eh? With the help of *your* magic? (*He roars with laughter then snarls harshly*) You addle-pated old has-been. Your magic is no match for that of Crunchbones. He could destroy you with one snap of his fingers. (*He snaps his fingers*)

Mother Goose (*smiling*) That may be so. But understand
The question won't arise.
Quick thought and simple cunning will
Cut Ogre Crunchbones down to size.
For though in magic he be versed,
He's pompous and conceited
And in the end you'll see by his
Own powers he'll be defeated.

Mother Goose exits R

Gruesome (*calling after her*) Don't make me laugh. (*Thoughtfully*) And yet—and yet. Perhaps I'd better warn him? If the tales I've heard are true, she *could* be dangerous. (*Glancing off* R) Farewell, friend Cat and Master Peter. Your lives are safe for the moment. But don't think you've seen the last of me. As soon as I've warned the Ogre, I promise I'll return to deal with *you*.

Gruesome laughs harshly and exits DL *as:*

The Chamberlain enters UL

Chamberlain (*calling*) Hallo-o? (*Looking around*) Is anybody there? (*Sigh-*

ing) Oh, dear, dear. This is the most *ridiculous* thing she's ever ordered me to do. Fancy riding around the countryside looking for a talking cat. Hallo-o?

The Chamberlain exits DR

Puss enters R. *He is carrying Peter's clothes in a bundle*

(*Off*) Mr Boots?

Puss (*gazing off down* R) Looks like we were just in time. Now to get rid of *these* old things and put the *next* part of my plan into operation. (*Dramatically*) What a strain it is, being a genius.

Puss exits CL

The Queen enters UL, *with an unhappy looking Princess*

Freckles follows. He is wearing a large coachman's coat over his costume

Queen Ooh, I say, what a lovely bit of countryside. As soon as we've met this Marquis of Carabosse, we can get the picnic basket out of the coach and have a nice spot of lunch. Oooh, and wait till you see what I've packed. There's a rhubarb and senna pod quiche, some home-made syrup of fig biscuits, two bottles of prune juice, and a great big chocolate cake with Ex-Lax topping. That ought to keep us going for a bit.

Princess Do we *really* have to stay here, Mother? Couldn't we go back to the village and have lunch there?

Queen (*surprised*) Certainly not. It's ages since I had a day in the country, and I want to enjoy it. Don't you, Freckles?

Freckles No, I don't. The last time *I* was out in the country, I ended up with a swollen nose through sniffing wild broses.

Queen (*blinking*) Wild *broses*?

Freckles That's right. Them pink flowers with thorns all over 'em. Broses.

Queen No, no, no, no, no. You mean *roses*. There's no "B" in roses.

Freckles There was in the one *I* sniffed. (*He yelps*) Owwwww. (*He clasps his neck*)

Princess (*startled*) What is it?

Freckles (*anguished*) I've just been stung by another one. (*He glances around*)

Queen Quick. Dab some iodine on it.

Freckles (*groaning*) Too late. It'll be miles away by now.

Queen (*looking around*) I wonder where the Chamberlain is?

The Chamberlain enters

Chamberlain Here I am, Your Majesty, but there's no sign of a talking cat anywhere. Are you *sure* you weren't mistaken?

Queen Of course I'm sure. We were going to meet him right here. (*Worried*) Oh, I say, you don't think he's been in an accident, do you?

Freckles How should I know? I've never had an accident in my life.

Queen What about last week then? When that dog bit you? Wasn't that an accident?

Freckles Course not. He did it on purpose.
Princess (*looking off* L) Look. Somebody's coming.

Puss enters, apparently in great distress

Puss (*excitedly*) Oh Your Majesty ... Your Majesty. Thank goodness you've arrived. My poor master ...
Queen (*alarmed*) What about him?
Puss There he was, minding his own business and inspecting his Estates, when two vicious villains attacked him, stole his beautiful clothes and threw him into yonder lake. (*He indicates* R)

All react with dismay

Princess How awful.
Puss I *beg* you to help him.
Queen Of course we will. (*To Freckles*) Quick, Freckles, down to the lake and give him a hand.

Freckles and Puss exit R

Oh, what a good job we came this way. Fancy the poor Marquis being attacked by robbers.
Chamberlain (*shaking his head*) I can't understand it. That's the second crime we've had in Arcadia since yesterday.
Princess Really? What was the first?
Queen A crackpot tried to blow up the Prime Minister's car.

The Princess reacts

But don't worry—it didn't work. He burnt his mouth on the exhaust pipe.

Puss enters R

Puss Your Majesty—(*bowing low*) allow me to present my master—The Marquis of Carabosse.

Peter enters nervously. He is now wearing the Coachman's coat previously worn by Freckles

Freckles follows Peter on

Peter (*bowing awkwardly*) Your Majesty.
Princess (*recognizing him*) Peter.
Peter (*recognizing her*) You.
Queen (*to the Princess*) Do you two know each other?
Princess (*happily*) Of course we do, Mother. It's the boy who saved my life yesterday morning.
Chamberlain (*puzzled*) But you told us *he* was a *miller's* son, Your Highness.
Puss (*quickly*) Oh—that was one of my master's *jokes*. He often pretends to be poor when he visits the towns and villages. If people knew he was the richest man in the world, he'd never have a minute's peace.

Peter reacts

Freckles That's true. My dad once won the football pools and for the first few days, he didn't know what to do about the begging letters.

Queen So what *did* he do?

Freckles Well—he thought it over, and then decided to keep sending 'em.

Peter (*firmly*) I'm sorry, Your Majesty, but I've got to tell you the truth——

Puss (*quickly*) He's absolutely *starving*. He hasn't had a thing to eat since breakfast and the fresh air gives him *such* an appetite.

Queen (*beaming*) Of course. We'll get the baskets out of the coach and have a picnic lunch. (*To Peter*) Then the Chamberlain can pop down to—(*local gents outfitters*) and get him some decent clothes to wear.

Peter (*protesting*) But——

Queen (*airily*) Oh, it's no trouble. I always carry an American Express Card tucked inside my corsets.

Princess (*hurrying to Peter*) You *will* accept, won't you? (*Appealingly*) Please.

Peter (*disarmed*) Well—if you *insist*.

Princess Oh, I *do*. I really do.

Queen (*beaming*) Then that's settled. Here—and I'll tell you what, we'll open a few bottles of champagne and have a little toast. To our new-found friends, the Marquis of Carabosse and his gallant Squire, Mr *Puss in Boots*.

All cheer and led by the Queen, begin to sing

Song 10 (Company)

As the song begins:

Marjory, Jack and the Chorus enter and the song continues to a rousing Finale to the First Act

CURTAIN

ACT II

Scene 1

The Gardens of the Royal Palace

A beautiful garden with fountains, statues, flowering shrubs, etc., and the Palace as a background. A white painted garden bench is c. *Graceful trees conceal entrances and exits* L *and* R

When the scene begins, Courtiers in splendid clothes are singing and dancing

Song and Dance (Courtiers)

At the end of the song all fall back into small groups as:

The Queen enters UR, *followed by Freckles*

The Courtiers bow and curtsey as:

The Queen and Freckles move DC

Queen (*beaming*) Oooh, I say everybody, you'll never guess what? Me daughter's fallen in love with that Marquis of Carabosse and wants to marry him.

The Courtiers react with pleasure

Mind you, I don't blame her. I mean, she'd have to be crackers to let *him* escape. (*Chortles*) Oooh, young—good-looking—rich—intelligent—everything a girl could wish for. (*Wistfully*) Reminds me of *my* first husband. What a man *he* was. Used to spend all his free time going up mountains.

Freckles (*startled*) Mountains?

Queen Oh, yes, did it for *years*. Then one day he kissed me goodbye—and set off for Mount Everest with the Wimpey expedition.

Freckles I didn't know Wimpeys had tried to reach the top of Mount Everest. Did they manage it?

Queen (*disgustedly*) No, they got half way up and ran out of scaffolding. But never mind about that, if Miranda and the Marquis *are* going to start thinking about getting married, *we'd* better have a word about *our* nuptials, hadn't we? (*She beams at him*)

Freckles (*reacting*) Oh, er—couldn't we do it later, Fanny? I mean, we don't want to rush things, do we? And besides . . . (*He indicates the crowd behind them*)

Queen (*cheerfully*) Oh, we can soon get rid of *them*. (*To the Courtiers*) Off you go, everyone. Freckles wants to be *alone* with me. (*She simpers*)

The Courtiers exit, with knowing smiles

(*To Freckles*) Now then, let's sit on that seat and get down to business. *I* think we should get married early in the morning. Don't you? About half past six.

Freckles (*amazed*) What do you want to get married at half past six for?

Queen Well, if things don't work out, we won't have wasted the whole day, will we?

Freckles (*protesting*) But—but—I can't marry you yet, Fanny. Not till I get a job.

Queen (*surprised*) But you've got a job. You work for me.

Freckles I know, but I don't want to be a page boy all me life. I want to do something *exciting*. As a matter of fact, I went for a new job this morning as a signal-man for British Rail. And you'll never guess what.

Queen No, I don't suppose I will.

Freckles I had to do a test for 'em. They asked me what I'd do if I was all alone in me signal box and I suddenly saw two trains rushing towards each other at top speed on the same railway track.

Queen (*curious*) And what did you say?

Freckles I said I'd pull the lever and switch one of 'em on to another track.

Queen (*relieved*) Well that's a relief.

Freckles "Ah, but what if the lever was stuck and you couldn't do that?" they asked me. "Simple," I said, "I'd grab a little red flag, run onto the track and wave it in front of them like this". (*He waves his imaginary flag vigorously*)

Queen Quite right. I'd do the same thing meself.

Freckles "Yes, but what if the drivers weren't looking and didn't see you?" they said. "Well in that case," I told 'em, "I'd dash home and get my little brother." "Why?" they said. "What would your little brother do?" "Nothing," I told 'em, "but he loves to watch train crashes."

Queen (*after a reaction*) Well you wouldn't get *me* travelling by train. All these train robberies have put me right off.

Freckles (*amused*) Train robberies? There's no train robberies these days.

Queen (*drily*) Have *you* bought a cup of tea and a sandwich in a British Rail Buffet Car recently?

The Chamberlain enters UR

Chamberlain (*moving down to them*) Ah, there you are, Your Majesty. There's a man at the door wishing to see you regarding sponsorship.

Queen Sponsorship?

Chamberlain (*nodding*) He's hoping to cross the Atlantic Ocean on a plank of wood.

Freckles (*scornfully*) Give over, he'll never find one long enough.

Queen (*after a reaction*) Well, I suppose we'd better see him. Lead on, Chamberlain.

The Chamberlain exits UR, *followed by the Queen and Freckles, as they vanish from view:*

Gruesome enters DL *and watches them go*

Gruesome (*sneering*) The fools. They're so delighted with this mysterious Marquis of Carabosse, they've relaxed their guard and enabled me to sneak into the grounds unseen. (*He chuckles*) How cunning is my master the Ogre. If I capture the Princess and carry her off, the price of her ransom shall be a prisoner each day, delivered to his Castle in chains, ready for him to eat, Then when everyone in Arcadia is gone—the Princess herself shall join them. (*He roars with laughter*) But now to find a suitable hiding place and take her by surprise.

Gruesome exits DL, *with a nasty chuckle as:*

Puss enters UR *in very good humour*

Puss Well, I think everything's turned out fine. Thanks to me, not only does everyone in the Palace think Master Peter is the Marquis of Carabosse, richest man on earth, but he's also got a set of fine new clothes and a princess who wants to marry him. (*Sobering*) Mind you, I've still got *one* more problem to solve. Queen Fanny wants to visit his Castle and look over the Estates, and unless I can talk her out of it, we could be in real trouble. (*He yawns*) Still, I'll worry about that later. Right now I could do with forty winks. All this thinking is making me sleepy. (*He yawns again and glances* C) *Those* bushes look inviting. Perhaps I can curl up under them for a while.

Puss exits CR, *yawning as:*

Caspar and Hector enter UL *cautiously*

Caspar (*softly*) Mr Gruesome. (*Slightly louder*) Mr Gruesome.
Hector (*glancing around*) He's not here.
Caspar (*irritated*) Of course he's here, fathead. We followed him from the village, didn't we? Saw him sneak past the guards.
Hector Yes, but he could have sneaked out again while we were trying to climb over the wall.
Caspar And whose fault is that, eh? It's *yours*. We wouldn't have *had* to climb the wall if you'd have hurried yourself. We could have caught up with him.
Hector Yes, I know but somebody pinched my wallet. I had to chase him all round the village, down the High Street, through the market, and past the bus station. Then just as I was catching up with him, he ran into the— (*local cinema*). You know, the one where they're showing—(*popular film*).
Caspar And did you follow him?
Hector Course I didn't.
Caspar Why not?
Hector I've seen it six times already.

Caspar pushes him violently as:

Gruesome enters DL

Gruesome (*angrily*) Bah, what are *you* idiots doing here?

Caspar You told us to let you know as soon as we'd kidnapped somebody.

Hector And we have done. We've kidnapped Marjory Daw.

Gruesome (*raging*) Fools. Dolts. Imbeciles. I didn't mean you'd to follow me *here*. If anyone sees us, we'll be thrown into the dungeons. Get back to the village and wait for me there. (*He glances off* R) Quickly, someone's coming.

Hector and Caspar quickly exit UL *as:*

Gruesome exits DL *as:*

The Princess enters R, *followed by Peter who is now dressed in rich velvet and satins*

Princess (*happily*) Oh Peter, I can't believe how different you look in your new clothes. No-one would ever guess you're not a *real* Marquis.

Peter (*wryly*) I suppose not, but now I've told *you* the truth, I wish you'd let me tell your *mother*, too.

Princess (*aghast*) Oh, you mustn't. She'd never let us marry if she knew you were only a *Miller's* son. She wants me to marry a prince, you see—or at least someone *rich*.

Peter (*stunned*) Then what are we going to do? I haven't a penny in the world.

Princess Don't worry. I'd rather marry a poor man I loved than a rich man I *didn't*.

Peter (*despairingly*) But the only thing I own is Puss. Even these clothes are borrowed. (*Sadly*) It's no use, Miranda. We'll *have* to tell her the truth.

Princess (*protesting*) But you won't be poor for long. The old fortune teller *promised* you fame and fortune. You *told* me she did.

Peter (*smiling wistfully*) That's true. I just wish I could *believe* it.

Princess (*firmly*) Well *I* do. I believe it with all my heart. And even if I'm wrong, I know there's no other person in the world I'd rather share my life with.

Song 12 (Princess and Peter)

At the end of the song:

The Chamberlain enters UR, *followed by a worried looking Jack Spratt. The Chamberlain indicates the Princess and Peter then exits again*

Peter (*surprised*) Jack, what are *you* doing here?

Jack It's Marjory Daw. She's vanished.

Peter (*surprised*) What?

Jack We can't find her anywhere. You've got to help us.

Princess Of course we will.

Puss enters UR *tiredly*

Puss (*protesting*) Can't a fellow get *any* rest in this place? What's the excitement?

Peter Something's happened to Marjory.

Jack No-one's seen her since last night, and the only trace we *did* find was her empty picnic basket at the foot of the bridge.

Puss (*with eyes opening wide*) Oh, my paws and whiskers. So it *wasn't* a dream.

Everyone looks at him in surprise

It happened a few minutes ago. I didn't take much notice because I thought I was asleep, but Caspar and Hector were telling old Gruesome they'd *kidnapped* her.

Everyone reacts

Jack (*startled*) What? Oh, you must be mistaken. I know they're sly and lazy, but they'd never *kidnap* anyone.

Peter All the same, it won't do any harm to ask a few questions. Let's go find them. (*To the Princess*) I'll be back as soon as we know she's safe. (*To Jack*) Come on, Jack. And don't worry, we'll find her wherever she is.

Peter, Jack and Puss exit UR *as:*

Gruesome appears cautiously and creeps up behind the Princess. With a cry of triumph, he gags her with one hand and clasps her about the waist with the other

Gruesome Aha, my pretty one. Got you at last. (*He laughs*)

The Princess struggles wildly but in vain

Now to return to my master's Castle in the middle of the Great Forest where you'll enjoy the tender hospitality of *Crunchbones the Ogre.*

Gruesome drags the struggling Princess off DL, *roaring with laughter*

Rapid fade to Black-out

Scene 2

A quiet street. A lane scene

As before

Freckles enters R, *laughing helplessly. For a few moments he continues to rock with laughter, then sobers and stands, face blank, as if in concentration. After a moment he shakes his head*

Freckles Rubbish. Rubbish. (*Once more he stands blank faced for a few moments then shrieks with laughter again, clutching his sides helplessly. After a few moments, he sobers and stands blank faced again*)

Queen Fanny enters R *in a resplendent new gown beaming at the audience*

(*Loudly*) Rubbish. Rubbish.

Startled, the Queen looks at him as he stands blank faced again, not seeing her. She then looks at the audience questioningly

(*Loudly*) Rubbish. Absolute rubbish. (*He goes blank faced*)

The Queen looks at him again uneasily

Suddenly Freckles shrieks with laughter and falls about

The Queen steps away from him wearing a worried look

(*Seeing her and sobering*) Oh, hallo, Fanny. What are *you* doing here?

Queen What am *I* doing here? You mean what are *you* doing? I was just going to send for the men in white coats.

Freckles Eh? (*Realizing*) Oh, you mean just then. No, no, there's nothing wrong with me. (*He gives a little laugh*) I was just telling meself a few jokes.

Queen (*blankly*) Jokes? Well what were you shouting, "Rubbish" for?

Freckles Oh, they were the ones I'd heard before.

The Queen double takes

Anyway you still haven't told me what you're doing here.

Queen Well, it's a bit *embarrassing*. (*She glances around to see no-one is near*) I was walking down the street, you see, and I saw this feller coming towards me carrying a *shotgun*. "Oh," I thought, "there's going to be a wedding." (*To the audience*) Well, you *would*, wouldn't you? (*To Freckles*) So I popped into—(*local card shop*) and bought a big box of confetti, and ooh, was my face *red*. I'd thrown half a box at him before I found out I'd made a mistake.

Freckles You mean, it wasn't a wedding at all?

Queen No, it was a Bank Robbery. (*Thoughtfully*) Mind you, talking about weddings—it has crossed my mind we might be rushing it a bit with *ours*. I mean, maybe we should wait a bit longer before we take the plunge, so to speak? What do *you* think?

Freckles (*eagerly*) Oh, yes. Good idea. Quite agree.

Queen The only thing is—it's supposed to be unlucky to postpone a wedding.

Freckles (*scornfully*) Course it isn't. (*Aside*) Not if you *keep* postponing it.

Queen And in any case we still haven't discussed where to go for the honeymoon.

Freckles Er, how about St Slithering-in-the-Swamp? I won a competition there last year—The Most Handsome Man in Town. (*He smirks*)

Queen (*eyeing him*) I think I'd prefer somewhere a bit more *crowded*. (*Brightly*) I know, let's take the Royal Yacht and go on a cruise.

Freckles Oh, Fanny, you know I don't like going on ships. I can't tell Port from Starboard.

Queen Don't be silly. There's nothing to it. All you've got to do is look at the labels on the bottles. (*Excitedly*) Oooh, *yes*. It'll be absolutely perfect—and we can take everybody else with us as well because there's *plenty* of room.

Freckles But—but where will we go?

Queen (*gaily*) Who cares, as long as we enjoy ourselves?

Song 13 (Queen and Freckles)

At the end of the song, the Queen and Freckles exit R

Hector and Caspar enter L, *looking rather annoyed*

Caspar Of all the dirty tricks.

Hector Yeah, and after all the trouble *we* went to. (*Indignantly*) Oooh, I just *knew* we couldn't trust that feller. He tells more lies than a politician at election time. He *promised* us that will, didn't he?

Caspar Yes, and now he's got Marjory Daw *and* the Princess, and we've got nothing.

Hector I've got a good mind to follow him to that Ogre's Castle and punch him right on the nose.

Caspar Good idea. (*Realizing*) Just a minute. Just a minute. What do you mean, you've got a good mind to go and punch him on the nose? He'd make mincemeat out of you.

Hector No he wouldn't. I'm a good *boxer*, I am. Don't you remember that time I entered the Golden Gloves Competition—and after I'd done eight rounds with—(*well known boxer*), they gave me a big cup? (*He preens himself*)

Caspar Yes, and every one of your teeth was inside it. (*Pushing him*) Idiot. We don't go anywhere *near* that Castle. We stay right here in the village and pretend we know nothing at all about any disappearances. Understand? If anybody finds out we know what's happened we'll be in big trouble.

Jack and Peter enter R

Peter (*grimly*) Oh? And what *has* happened?

Caspar and Hector react in fright

Come on. Out with it. (*He grabs Hector by the collar*)

Hector (*wailing*) It wasn't our fault. It was Gruesome.

Caspar (*nodding furiously*) *He's* the one who did it.

Jack (*grimly*) The one who did *what*?

Hector (*fearfully*) The one who kidnapped the Princess. He's just driven off with her in a big black coach. (*He indicates* L)

Peter (*astounded*) But that's *impossible*. We left her in the Palace Gardens.

Caspar Maybe you did, but Marjory Daw's with him, too. He's going to feed them to the Ogre for his dinner.

Peter (*horrified*) What?

Jack (*urgently*) We've got to save them, Peter. I'll find the Guards.

Peter There isn't time. We'll have to do it ourselves. Come on. (*He tugs at Hector and moves* L *to exit*)

Hector (*startled and pulling back*) Eh? You must be joking.

Caspar You don't catch *us* hanging about the Ogre's Castle. It's full of ghosts and things.

Peter (*grimly*) Is that so? Well, ghosts or no ghosts, you're coming with us. There's something odd about all this and we're not letting you out of our sight until Marjory and the Princess are safe. Now move.

Peter pulls the protesting Hector off L *and is followed by a reluctant Caspar, driven by Jack*

Puss enters R

Puss (*relieved*) Thank goodness my hearing's nice and sharp. If I'd been here a moment earlier, they'd have wanted *me* to go with them, too. (*He shudders*) I know I've got nine lives, but the quickest way to lose them all is by upsetting Crunchbones the Ogre. I'm sorry, Master Peter, I'd like to help you rescue them, but this is one time I'm going to keep my nose out of things.

Mother Goose enters R

Mother Goose (*sternly*) Is *this* the way you show your thanks
　　　　　　　　To those you're meant to serve?
　　　　　　　　If so . . . then power of speech and youth
　　　　　　　　Is much, much more than you deserve.
　　　　　　　　Perhaps, it would be better if
　　　　　　　　To save you further strain
　　　　　　　　I changed you back into a
　　　　　　　　Common house-cat once again? (*She raises her wooden
　　　　　　　　　spoon*)
Puss But—but—I can't fight an *Ogre*, Mother Goose. Especially *this* one. He's bigger than a house and has magic powers too.
Mother Goose (*scornfully*) And has the brain inside your head
　　　　　　　　With terror taken wing?
　　　　　　　　Remember, e'en the tiniest bee
　　　　　　　　When roused, can give a nasty sting.
　　　　　　　　Young David killed Goliath, and
　　　　　　　　St George, the Dragon slew . . .
　　　　　　　　Have courage and you'll find
　　　　　　　　There's simply nothing you can't do.

Song 14 (Mother Goose with Puss)

At the end of the song:

Mother Goose exits R

Puss (*excitedly to the audience*) She's right. There *is* nothing I can't do. So what if Crunchbones *is* a mile high? I'm smarter than *he* is. I've got brains I haven't even used yet. (*As he realizes*) And that's given me another idea—Queen Fanny wants to visit the Marquis' Estate, doesn't she? Well—so she *shall*. I'll tell her to summon the Royal Coach at once. (*He sings a reprise of the song*)

Puss exits L *brightly*

Fade to Black-out

SCENE 3

The Courtyard of Crunchbones' Castle. Early evening

The backdrop is the exterior of a huge castle. An arch leads into the courtyard
R, *and other exits and entrances are concealed by buttresses, etc.*

*The Courtyard is filled with evil spirits and goblins performing a wild and
frenetic dance*

Dance (Spirits and Goblins)

At the end of the dance, they exit quickly L *and* R:

*Gruesome enters through the arch, with the struggling Princess and Marjory
firmly in his grasp. He moves* C

Princess Let go of me. Let go.
Marjory (*calling*) Help. Help.
Gruesome (*amused*) Welcome to the Ogre's Castle. (*He releases them with
an evil laugh*)
Princess (*backing away from him*) Why have you brought us here?
Marjory Take us home at once.
Gruesome (*laughing*) Home? This *is* your home. From now on, you'll be
slaves of the Ogre and do his every bidding.
Princess (*defiantly*) Never.
Gruesome (*leering*) We shall see. My master has many ways of making you
change your minds.
Marjory We're not afraid of *him*.
Gruesome (*glancing off* L) Indeed? Then I suggest you tell him so—for here
he comes now.
Ogre (*off* L) Fee, fi, fo, fum.

The two girls retreat R *as:*

*Crunchbones the Ogre clomps grumbling and growling into the courtyard.
He is a monstrous being, some ten feet in height, and carries a huge wooden
staff (to give him additional support). He comes to a halt just* L *of* C *and
looks at the girls*

So—these are Arcadians, are they? (*He chuckles nastily*) And which is the
Princess Miranda?
Gruesome That one, O Master. (*He indicates the Princess*)
Ogre (*admiringly*) Hmmmmm. You chose well, Gruesome. She'll make a
dainty dish for supper when the time is right. (*To the Princess*) Come
closer, girl. I want to see you better. (*He reaches out to her*)
Princess (*recoiling from him*) Keep away from me, you horrible monster.
Marjory Leave her alone.
Ogre (*looking at Marjory*) And who are *you*?
Gruesome (*sneering*) Just a village girl, Master. No-one of importance.
Ogre I see. (*Fiercely*) Then take her to the kitchen and have her roasted for
my supper *tonight*.

Princess (*aghast*) No.
Gruesome But Master, had you forgotten? We have no Chef. You ate him
this morning for spoiling your breakfast.
Ogre (*annoyed*) Then find me *another* one.

Gruesome exits L, *with the struggling Marjory*

(*To the Princess*) And as for you, my pretty Princess, I shall see you again
at suppertime.

Crunchbones exits L, *with much grunting and muttering*

Princess (*despairingly*) Oh, what are we going to do? How can anyone save
us if they don't know where we are?

Peter and Jack cautiously enter through the arch. Both carry swords

Peter (*seeing her*) Miranda.
Princess (*turning*) Peter. (*She hurries to him*)

They embrace

Jack But where's Marjory?
Princess Inside the castle. They're going to roast her for the Ogre's supper
tonight. You've got to save her.
Jack Don't worry. We will.

Jack exits L *rapidly*

Princess Oh, Peter. We were so frightened. How on earth did you find us?
Peter I'll tell you later. The *important* thing is we're here and you're both
safe. By this time tomorrow, we'll all be home again and the Royal Army
will be on its way to deal with Crunchbones once and for all.
Princess Do you really mean that?
Peter Of course I do. From now on there isn't a thing to worry about.

Song 15 (Peter and Princess)

After the song the Ogre's voice is heard off L

Ogre Fe, Fi, Fo, Fum—I smell the blood of Arcadians.
Princess It's the Ogre. Quick. Hide.

The Princess and Peter exit DL *as:*

Crunchbones enters UL, *grunting and grumbling as usual*

Ogre (*suspiciously*) Strange, methought I heard voices. (*He looks around*)

Hector and Caspar enter through the arch

They are on tiptoe, and move DC *with exaggerated caution without noticing the
Ogre who is behind them, watching curiously*

Hector (*calling*) Coo-ee. Anybody home?
Caspar (*startled; hitting him*) Shhh. What do you want to go shouting like
that for? Somebody might hear us.

Hector Well, it's creepy out here with nobody with us. I keep thinking somebody's looking at me.

Caspar Don't be daft. Who'd want to look at *you*?

Hector (*indignantly*) How do you mean? I'm just as good looking as you are.

Caspar (*scornfully*) Give over.

Hector I *am*. 'Cos we're *brothers*, see. And both our faces came from the same mould.

Caspar Yes, but yours is a lot mouldier. (*He pushes him and laughs*)

Hector (*hurt*) Oh, well if you're going to be nasty to me, I shan't speak to you any more. (*He turns away and pouts*)

Caspar Oh, don't be daft. I was only pulling your leg. Come on. Say something.

Hector shakes his head

(*Coaxing*) Come on. *Please.*

Ogre (*with menace*) Fe, Fi, Fo, Fum.

Caspar (*surprised*) Pardon?

Ogre (*louder*) Fe, Fi, Fo, Fum.

Caspar Oh, come on. Talk English. (*He pushes Hector*)

Ogre (*very loudly*) Aghhhhh. (*He thumps his staff on the ground*)

Caspar and Hector turn to see him and react

Caspar |
Hector | (*together*) Aghhhhh. (*They cling to each other and scuttle* DL)

Hector It's the Jolly Green Giant. (*He holds his sides*) Ho, ho, ho.

Ogre (*annoyed*) I am Crunchbones the Ogre. King of all Ogres and Master of Magic.

Caspar (*to Hector*) Oh, he's a *conjurer*. Here, I wonder if he knows Paul Daniels? (*or other well-known magician*)

Ogre (*grimly*) So, you like a little joke, do you? Very well, tonight you shall join me for supper and we'll *all* have a laugh.

Hector (*pleased* Oh, thank you. We *are* a bit hungry, now you come to mention it. And what are you having for supper?

Ogre (*booming*) *You two.* (*He lifts his staff with a roar and pounds it again*)

Hector and Caspar yell with fright and exit L *rapidly, followed by the Ogre*

As they vanish from view:

Puss enters through the arch cautiously

Puss (*tiredly*) Oh my paws and whiskers. I've never run so fast in all my life. (*He glances off through the arch*) Still, there's no sign of the Royal Coach yet, so let's hope my little plan worked. (*To the audience*) Just a few miles down the road there's a huge field of corn, and I've persuaded the farmer to tell anyone who asks him, that it all belongs to his master, the Marquis of Carabosse. I did the same thing with a farmer who had a great herd of cattle, and one who had a flock of sheep, so with a bit of luck, all three of them will tell the same story. But now for the most *difficult* part. If I'm going to fool Queen Fanny into thinking this place belongs to him too, somehow I've got to get rid of old Crunchbones *and* his henchmen before she arrives. (*He glances off through the arch again*) Oh no, here she comes now. The coach is stopping and she's getting out. Mousetraps and Stilton. I've got to work fast.

Puss exits hurriedly

The Queen, Freckles and the Chamberlain enter

Queen (*brightly*) Oooh. Anybody ho-ome? (*Looking around*) Oh, I say, what a magnificent old castle. I wouldn't mind staying here for a few days, would you? It'd be perfect for a holiday.
Freckles (*blankly*) Eh?
Queen I said, "I wouldn't mind staying here for a holiday".

Freckles looks at her blankly

(*Exasperated*) Oh, come *on*. You know what a holiday *is*, don't you?
Freckles 'Course I do. It's when people go hundreds of miles to strange and exotic places so they can have their photographs taken in front of their cars.

The Queen double takes

Anyway, you wouldn't catch *me* spending me holidays here. There's nothing round here but trees. No, the next time *I* go on holiday, it'll be to the South Sea Islands and then I can go swimming every day in that lovely clear water. (*He makes swimming motions*)
Chamberlain (*clearing his throat*) Excuse me, Mr Freckles, but don't you think that would be rather *unwise*? I mean, those South Sea Islands are surrounded by man eating sharks.
Freckles Yes, I know. But they wouldn't touch *me*.
Queen (*surprised*) Why not?
Freckles (*proudly*) I've got a tattoo on me chest that protects me.
Queen (*in disbelief*) A tattoo?
Freckles Yes, it says "The best thing that ever happened to Britain was the Poll Tax", and even a *shark* won't swallow that.
Queen (*double takes*) What are you *talking* about? You don't even *know* how to swim.
Freckles (*indignantly*) Yes, I do. Me grandad taught me and *he* was a champion swimmer. He once did two hundred metres in ten seconds.
Chamberlain (*blinking*) But that's impossible.
Freckles Not it isn't. He went over a waterfall.
Chamberlain (*following a reaction*) Er, perhaps we should inform the Marquis we've arrived, Your Majesty?
Queen Good idea, Chamberlain. Off you go. Freckles and I want to look round the gardens before it gets too dark.

The Chamberlain bows and exits DL

Freckles What do we want to look round the gardens for?

Queen Well, they'll be full of flowers, won't they? And I *love* flowers. My late husband wore one in his lapel every day just to please *me*. Mind you, they caused him agony, poor thing.

Freckles Why? Did he have hay fever?

Queen No, the plantpots kept bruising his ribs.

Freckles (*after a reaction*) Oh, all right then. I'll walk you round the gardens till it gets dark. Here, and then perhaps we can pause and watch the moon come out, eh?

Queen Well, I don't mind watching the moon come out, but you can keep your *paws* to yourself. (*She chortles heartily*) No, I was only joking. As a matter of fact, it'll give us a chance to have a few minutes alone. (*She simpers*)

Freckles (*alarmed*) Eh? What for?

Queen Well, there's something I want to *ask* you. I mean, we've been going out together for months now, and I still don't know your last name.

Freckles Oh, I haven't got one.

Queen Of course you've got one. Everybody's got one. What are your parents called?

Freckles Mummy and Daddy.

Queen (*wincing*) No, no, you don't understand. You see when we get married, I want us to have a hyphenated name, 'cos it sounds a lot posher. You know—like Ponsonby-Smallpiece, or Jones-Higginbottom. Now *my* last name is *Eaton*, so we want something that goes in front of *that*, don't we?

Freckles Yes, how about moth?

Queen (*upset*) Oh, it's useless trying to talk to you. I don't think you want to get married at all. (*She sniffles*)

Freckles Oh, don't cry, Fanny. I was only kidding. Come on, give me a kiss.

Queen (*still sniffling*) I don't know that I should. I've never kissed a man before.

Freckles Neither have I, but don't let that stop you.

Song 16 (Freckles and Queen)

At the end of the song Freckles and the Queen exit DL

Rapid fade to Black-out

SCENE 4

Beneath the Ogre's Castle

A lane scene. The back cloth shows dank, stone walls and cobwebbed armour. If this is not possible, the scene can be played in front of plain tabs. It is very dim and gloomy

Caspar and Hector enter at opposite sides, with their backs to each other. With exaggerated steps they move C *and collide. With shrieks of alarm they turn and see each other*

Hector (*clutching at his heart*) Oooh, thank goodness it's you. I thought it was the King of the Sumo Wrestlers.

Caspar Me too. (*Looking around*) I wonder where we are?

Hector I don't know, but it's real scary, isn't it? Did you see that room down the corridor with all those dead bodies in it?

Caspar Dead bodies?

Hector Yes, they were all sitting in chairs round a big table, cold and stiff, mouths open and eyes gazing into space. (*He shudders*) Oooh, it was horrible.

Caspar (*pushing him*) Idiot. They weren't dead bodies. That was a meeting of—(*local Town Council*)

The Queen, Freckles and Chamberlain enter L

Queen (*relieved*) Oh, thank goodness we've found someone. We've been wandering around the corridors for ages.

Hector Blimey, it's Queen Fanny and the Royal party. What are *you* doing here?

Freckles We've come for a look round but we seem to have got ourselves lost.

Caspar Us too. And it's not very nice down here, is it? If you ask me, I think this place is haunted.

Chamberlain (*startled*) Haunted? (*Looking around in fright*) Oh dear, and I haven't brought a torch with me.

Freckles What do you want a torch for?

Chamberlain Well, I read in a book once, that if you carried a torch, ghosts couldn't catch you. Do you think it's true?

Queen It depends how fast you can carry the torch. (*She laughs*) Oh, you are silly, Chamberlain. There's no such thing as ghosts.

Hector Oh, yes there are. Caspar and me once stayed in a haunted house, and in the middle of the night a horrible ghost came through the wall just as if the wall wasn't there.

Chamberlain (*awed*) And what did you *do*?

Caspar We went through the opposite wall in exactly the same way.

Freckles (*smugly*) Well, ghosts and things don't scare *me*.

Queen Oooh, you big fibber. You told me you were too scared to sleep at night in case there was a monster hiding under the bed.

Freckles Yes, I know. But I cured myself, didn't I?

Chamberlain (*interested*) How?

Freckles I sawed the legs off the bed.

Hector (*suddenly*) Here, I've had an idea.

Caspar Beginner's luck.

Hector Just in case there *is* something nasty down here, why don't we sing a little song? Ghosties and ghoulies don't like music, you know. It scares them away.

Chamberlain (*quickly*) Brilliant idea. What shall we sing?

Caspar Er, "She was only a farmer's daughter, but she had the best calves in town"?

Freckles No, no, there's too many verses in that one. How about something

from a *musical*? You know, a song from that show about the "clumsy
weightlifter"

Queen (*puzzled*) "Clumsy weightlifter"?

Freckles Yes, *Careless Rupture*.

Hector Oh, let's sing something we *all* know, *Side by Side*.

Chamberlain Yes, and if the boys and girls out there see anything nasty
hanging around, they can shout and warn us, can't they?

Queen Good idea. And if they shout loud enough—I'll lengthen the school
holidays. (*To the Musical Director*) Thank you, Mr Pianist.

They begin to sing

    After a moment a frightful monster (or ghost) lurches on L, *crossing behind
them to exit* R

The singers stop as:

The audience reacts

Freckles (*concerned*) What's the matter? What is it?

By-play with the audience

Queen A monster? Oh, I say, I don't like the sound of that. (*She looks
around*) Where did it go?

Audience reaction

Chamberlain (*nervously*) Perhaps we'd better take a look?

Hector Good idea.

*To the accompaniment of creepy music, they tiptoe cautiously in a rough circle
before ending up in their original places*

Caspar They're pulling our legs. There's nothing there.

Freckles We'll start again.

They sing again

    The Monster crosses behind them R *to* L *and exits*

The singers grind to a halt as:

The audience react

Queen What is it? What are you shouting for?

Audience by-play with ad-libs by singers

Chamberlain (*finally*) Well *I* think we should have another look round.

Hector Yes and we'll go the other way this time.

*With the musical accompaniment, they tiptoe around again in the opposite
direction, ending in their original positions*

Freckles (*disgustedly*) They're having us on. There's nobody there at all.

Caspar Let's carry on singing.

They sing once more

   The Monster enters L and moves behind them

Audience reaction and the singers stop singing once more

Queen What is it *now*?

By-play with the audience

Chamberlain (*shocked*) A monster *behind* us?

Audience reaction

Hector (*nervously*) Per-per-per-perhaps we'd better have a look?
Freckles (*nodding*) We'll count up to three, then we'll all turn and grab it.
  Right?
All (*except the Monster*) Right. One. Two.

The Monster ducks down

   Three. (*They turn quickly, but see nothing. Disgustedly they turn back to
   face the audience*)

The Monster stands again

Caspar That's done it. We're not taking any more notice of that lot.
Queen Quite right. (*To the audience*) You're all very naughty. (*To the
  others*) Come on everybody. We'll carry on with our song.

They begin singing

*The Monster taps Hector on the shoulder. He turns, sees it, laughs, nudges
Caspar and points towards the Monster*

Caspar looks and also laughs

   *Caspar and Hector continue singing. Suddenly they realize what they have
   seen, react in terror and exit rapidly pursued by the Monster*

*The Queen, the Chamberlain and Freckles realize they are gone and stop
singing*

Freckles (*looking around*) Hey, where've they gone to? We haven't finished
  the song yet.
Queen Oh, never mind. It didn't sound very good as a quintet, did it? It'll
  sound much better as a trio. Let's carry on singing.

They sing again

   The Monster enters and taps the Chamberlain's shoulder

   *The Chamberlain turns, reacts and exits at top speed followed by the
   Monster*

The Queen and Freckles grind to a halt and look round

Freckles Here? What's happened to him?

Queen I don't know. (*Slightly worried*) Perhaps there *is* something strange
about this place?

Freckles (*scornfully*) 'Course there isn't. Let's carry on singing.

The Queen and Freckles sing

    The Monster enters and taps Freckles

    Freckles reacts and exits chased by the Monster

The Queen falters then stops singing

Queen Freckles? (*Looking round nervously*) Freckles? (*Alarmed*) Oo-er.
Now *he's* gone as well. Mind you, he never did like classical singers. I
remember telling him once I'd paid thousands of pounds to be taught how
to sing properly and he said he'd better introduce me to his brother. I said,
"Why? Is *he* a singer as well?" And he said, "No, he's a lawyer. He'll get
your money back for you." Cheeky monkey. Anyway, now there's
nobody here but us, I'll show you how a *real* singer can sing. (*She begins
singing again*)

    The Monster enters and taps the Queen's shoulder

The Queen looks round

    The Monster screams and exits

Quick Black-out

SCENE 5

The Ogre's kitchen

*A pantomime kitchen with a boiler, fire, oven and shelving painted on the
backdrop. A kitchen table is up just R of C, and on it stands a pastry bowl, a
bag of flour, and mixing spoon and a box of eggs. Inside the bowl are several
artificial soft "dumplings". Hanging on hooks at the side of the table are a fly-
swat and a large frying pan. Behind the table is an artificial flower in a plant-
pot*

*When the scene begins, Assistant Cooks are singing and dancing as they move
around carrying Oxo cubes, buckets of water, salt packets, vegetables, etc., all
being of gigantic size*

Gruesome, whip in hand, stands DR, watching them

Song 17 (Cooks)

*During the course of the song, their burdens are carried offstage L and R and
deposited. At the end of the song, the Ogre's voice is heard off L*

Ogre (*off*) Fe, Fi, Fo, Fum.

All the Assistant Cooks fall to their knees and hang their heads as:

Crunchbones enters muttering and grumbling

(*Loudly*) What's all the noise about? And where's my supper?
Gruesome Patience, Master. The new chefs will be here in a moment.
Ogre Chefs?
Gruesome That's right, Master. Two of them. I found them wandering around the castle a few minutes ago.
Ogre (*sourly*) Good. Then see they begin work at once. And as for the rest of you—get back to work and don't let me hear another sound or I'll have *you* for supper too. (*He bangs his staff on the ground*)

The Assistant Cooks jump to their feet and scurry off

(*To Gruesome*) Now bring me some wine from the cellars, and after that prepare the girl. I want her cooked to perfection and served with roast potatoes and plenty of vegetables.
Gruesome Yes, Master.

Gruesome exits DR *as:*

The Ogre exits L *muttering and grumbling as usual as:*

Caspar and Hector enter UR. *They are wearing oversized chef outfits and both sport fake moustaches*

Hector (*nervously*) Here, you don't think he recognized us, do you? That Gruesome feller?
Caspar 'Course he didn't. *Nobody* could recognize us in these outfits. We look just like real chefs.
Hector Yes, but we don't know anything *about* cooking, do we?
Caspar You speak for yourself. Inside *my* head are recipes fit for a King.
Hector (*scornfully*) Give over. The last time you made *beans on toast*, you got the tin stuck in the toaster. Even *I* know more about cooking than you do.
Caspar All right then. All right. What do you know about foreign dishes?
Hector They break just as easily as English ones.
Caspar (*wincing*) Oh, come on. Let's see what we can whip up.

Caspar and Hector move C *and go behind the table*

Right. We'll start off with a Yorkshire Pudding.
Hector Oooh, I love Yorkshire Pudding.
Caspar First of all, we need a little flour.
Hector A little flower. (*He stoops down and picks up the flower in a plant-pot*)
Caspar Not *that* kind of flower, fathead. (*He plunges his hand into the flour bag and brings a handful out*) This kind. (*He tosses it in Hector's face*)

Hector splutters and blows the loose flour away as Caspar tips flour into the bowl

Now then . . . Beat me some eggs.

Hector opens the egg box, picks up the fly-swat and proceeds to attack the eggs

What are you doing? What are you doing? (*He snatches the fly-swat*)

Hector Beating the eggs.
Caspar (*wearily*) Why don't you grow up, stupid?
Hector I have done.
Caspar (*annoyed*) Look at the mess. Look at it. Oh, never mind. Just tip it
into the bowl. (*He puts the fly-swat down*)

Hector tips the egg-box and all into the bowl

   Right. *Now add the water.*
Hector Add the water. Add the water. (*He looks round*) Where's the water?
Caspar *I* don't know, do I? Go and find some.

   Hector exits L

Caspar picks up the spoon and begins to mix the flour and eggs

   Hector enters carrying a soda syphon

Hector I'm back.
Caspar (*without looking*) Have you got the water?
Hector I've got the water.
Caspar Right. Let me have it.

Hector looks at the audience and grins

Hector (*to the audience*) Shall I?

Audience reaction

   (*To Caspar*) You don't *really* want it, do you?
Caspar (*still mixing*) Of course I want it, fathead. *Give* it to me, will you?
Give it to me.
Hector You asked for it. (*He aims the syphon at him and lets fly*)

Caspar howls and covers his face. Hector doubles up with laughter

Caspar (*grimly*) Oh, you thought that was funny, did you? Well let's see you
laugh *this* off.

*Caspar snatches the syphon, aims at Hector, but fails to notice the nozzle is
pointing at himself. He squeezes the trigger and gets a second soaking*

Hector laughs

*Furious, Caspar puts the syphon down, and picks up the frying pan. As he
rushes towards Hector, Hector dashes behind the table*

Hector (*panic stricken*) Geroff. Geroff. (*He dips his hand into the bowl and
grabs a dumpling which he throws at Caspar*)

Caspar bats it with the frying pan

Hector continues to pelt Caspar who sends them flying into the audience

The Chamberlain suddenly enters R

Chamberlain (*horrified*) Gentlemen, Gentlemen, stop.

At once both Hector and Caspar stop and look innocent

Is *this* the way for the Marquis' chefs to behave? Let's sit down quietly
and have a nice cup of tea and some lemon meringue pie.

Caspar Lemon meringue pie?

Chamberlain Yes, there's a whole trayful on that shelf in the corridor. I'll go
and get them, shall I?

The Chamberlain exits

Caspar and Hector put down their weapons

*The Chamberlain enters with a trayful of large shaving-mousse pies on
paper plates*

(*Beaming*) Here we are. Lovely, lovely pies.

Hector Oh, I can't wait to get a mouthful of them.

Caspar (*picking one up*) Well have this one, then. (*He pushes it in Hector's
face and roars with laughter*)

*As the Chamberlain reacts with open-mouthed horror, with great deliberation,
Hector scrapes the mousse away, selects another pie, removes Caspar's hat,
places the pie on Caspar's head, replaces the hat, then smashes it down firmly
with the flat of his hand*

*After a reaction, Caspar unfastens Hector's coat, selects a pie, and lifting
Hector's shirt front, squashes the pie firmly on to his chest. He then releases
the shirt and wipes his hands in satisfaction*

*After a reaction, Hector unfastens Caspar's coat, selects a pie, pulls Caspar's
waistband away from his body and slides the pie down the front of his trousers*

As Caspar reacts, as an afterthought, Hector pats it firmly to squash it

Chamberlain (*finding his voice*) Now that is *enough*. Enough, I say.

*Caspar and Hector look at him, then at each other, nod, and each moves
toward the Chamberlain*

*Nervously, the Chamberlain watches them as they flank him and pick up the
remaining two pies*

Caspar and Hector face front, with their pies at the ready

Caspar ⎱
Hector ⎰ (*together*) One—Two—

Gruesome enters behind Chamberlain, carrying a great flagon of wine

Three.

Chamberlain ducks as:

Hector and Caspar whirl round and the pies hit Gruesome in the face

Hector, Caspar and the Chamberlain react and exit quickly R *as:*

Gruesome drops the flagon and howls with rage

Hearing the noise, several of the Assistant Cooks enter L

Gruesome (*scraping the mousse away and looking around*) Who did that?

The Cooks look blank

  Bah. Clear this mess away at once while I take this wine to the Ogre.

  As Gruesome picks up the flagon of wine and exits

  The Cooks pick up the table, etc. and carry it off

A moment later, Peter and the Princess enter cautiously DR

Peter (*calling softly*) Jack? Marjory? Are you there? (*Looking around*) Not a sign.

Princess (*concerned*) Oh Peter, he should never have set foot in here alone.

Peter Now stop worrying. I'm sure he's all right. It's a big place and they could be anywhere.

Princess But what if the Ogre's caught him?

Peter Then it's up to me to rescue him. Magic powers, or no magic powers, an Ogre's no match for a sharp sword.

  Mother Goose enters R

Mother Goose Alas, my friend, I fear you're wrong.
                Great care you need to take.
                Old Crunchbones is invincible
                'Gainst any weapon *mortals* make.

Peter (*surprised*) The old woman from the Fayre. What are *you* doing here?

Mother Goose I come to give you good advice.
                Put down the sword you wield.
                To someone else, this very night
                Shall mighty Ogre, Crunchbones, yield.
                His magic will avail him naught . . .
                (He'll soon discover that)
                When faced with gentle purring
                And the cunning of a talking cat.

  Mother Goose twirls her spoon and exits

Peter (*calling*) Wait, too late. She's gone again.

Princess But what did she mean? Puss can't fight an *Ogre*.

  Puss enters UL

Puss (*brightly*) Who says I can't?

Peter Puss. Where did *you* spring from?

Puss No time to talk now. The Ogre's heading this way, so you'd better hide yourself if my plan's going to work.

Ogre (*off* L) Fe, Fi, Fo, Fum.

Puss Quickly.

  Peter and the Princess exit DL, *ushered off by Puss*

  Puss scuttles DR *to take position*

  Crunchbones enters muttering and grumbling as usual

Ogre Gruesome. Gruesome. Where's my supper? (*He sees Puss*) Who are *you?*

Puss (*airily*) I, sir, am the personal valet of the Marquis of Carabosse. (*He bows*)

Ogre But you're a *cat.*

Puss At the moment, yes, but tomorrow I could be an elephant—or even a giraffe. It all depends how my Master feels. He's a great magician you see.

Ogre What?

Puss Oh yes, only yesterday he turned his car into a petrol station.

Ogre And what are you *doing* here?

Puss Well—he *was* thinking of adding this place to his collection—so I came to have a look round. But of course, he wouldn't want a sitting tenant, would he? He'll have to get rid of *you.*

Ogre (*astounded*) What? (*He snarls*) And how does he intend to do that, pray?

Puss By magic, of course. I told you he was a magician.

Ogre Bah, his magic is useless against *mine.* I am the greatest magician in the whole wide world.

Puss (*amused*) Really? I must remember to tell my master that. He likes a good laugh.

Ogre (*annoyed*) A laugh, eh? Then watch, and I'll prove it to you. (*He raises his arms and recites slowly at first but rising to a climax*)

As he speaks, the Lights dim to a total Black-out so that by the time his spell finishes, nothing at all can be seen

> Hocus-pokus, fiddle-de-fum, Presti-didgi-torium.
> Abra-cadabbacus, fiddle-I-fo. Manicus, panicus, vanicus-o.
> Heckerty-peckerty, faddle-de-fie. Via Germanicus, dabbicus, *AYE.*

Eerie music begins to play and a U.V. Fantasy Scene begins. This can be done as the Director or space permits, but the following may be of help

U.V. Fantasy Scene

A small fish painted in brilliant colours swims in R

It is followed a moment later by two more. They all exit R, *then enter hurriedly as:*

A shark with gaping mouth chases them. All exit L

A medium sized fish enters R *and moves lazily* L. *It suddenly turns about and heads* R *again quickly as:*

The shark returns and chases it off

Two swordfish enter, one L, *the other* R. *At once they circle each other and begin to fight a duel with their "swords". Suddenly they break off and exit rapidly as:*

The shark re-enters R *and glides around hungrily before exiting* L

A large sea-horse appears L, *followed by a smaller one and several tiny ones. All exit* R

A giant manta enters L, *its huge wings flapping gracefully. It circles the area before exiting* R

A medium-sized fish enters L *pushing a pram made of a clam shell. A baby fish with a feeding bottle in its mouth in the pram. They cross* R *and exit*

The seahorses enter R, *and cross to exit* L

A fishing hook on a line descends C

A medium-sized fish enters R *and examines it. The line jigs up and down. Swimming off* L, *the fish reappears with an old boot in its mouth. It hangs on the hook and the boot is drawn up*

The fish exits L

An orange octopus enters R, *and moves* C

Suddenly the shark re-enters R *and attacks*

The octopus produces a large mallet and beats the shark over the head with it

The shark exits R

The octopus exits L

The manta ray returns R, *and exits* L

The original small fishes enter L. *They exit* R *and the stage is empty once more*

The Lights go up to normal, but the U.V. remains on

Ogre Well, my feline friend, and what did you think of *that*, eh?

Puss (*airily*) Oh, ... I suppose it was all right for an *amateur*. But my Master the Marquis can do far more interesting things than produce a few fish. *He* can change *himself* into anything he wishes.

Ogre (*scornfully*) Bah, any magician can do that.

Puss Really? Well *he* could turn into a *lion* if he wanted.

Ogre So can I.

Puss (*scornfully*) I'd like to see you.

Ogre Very well—you *shall*. (*He raises his arms once more*) Hocus-pokus, fiddle-I-fo. Abra-cadabbacus, vanicus-o. Heckety-peckety, fiddle-de-fum. Presti-didgi-torium. Manicus, panicus, fiddle-de-fie. Via Germanicus, dabbicus *AYE*.

The Lights fade to Black-out

A loud roar is heard

Crunchbones quickly exits in the dark

Onto the stage springs a huge fierce looking U.V. lion

(*Off*) Is *this* what you wanted? (*He laughs harshly*)

Puss (*in the darkness*) W—w— well it's not *bad*—but I bet you couldn't change yourself into something smaller. A *mouse* for instance.
Ogre (*off; annoyed*) You doubt my powers? Then watch.

The lion vanishes

Puss (*heaving a sigh*) Well—I'm waiting.
Ogre (*off*) For what? I'm *here*, you stupid cat.
Puss Where? I can hardly see a thing in *this* light.
Ogre (*off*) Down on the floor, of course.
Puss Oh, I'm sorry. I'll have to have more light than this.
Ogre (*off*) Oh, very well. Let there be light, then.

The Lights return to normal and the U.V. is switched off

Now can you see me?
Puss (*peering at the ground*) Why, I do believe I *can*. (*He pounces on the "mouse"*)
Ogre (*off; in terror*) Aaaaaggh.

Puss pops the "mouse" in his mouth quickly and "eats" it

Puss And very tasty too. (*He dusts his hands*)

Gruesome enters DL *with Marjory*

Gruesome Here she is, Master. All ready to—(*He sees Puss*) You. (*Gruesome releases Marjory and draws his sword*)
Puss Oh-oh. (*He steps back in alarm*)
Gruesome I'll carve you into little pieces. (*He advances on Puss*)

Peter enters with the Princess behind him

Peter Not so fast, Gruesome. There's an old score *I* have to settle first. (*He draws his own sword*)

Gruesome spins round to face him

Gruesome We'll see about that. (*Calling loudly*) Master, Master, quickly.
Puss (*cheerfully*) I'm afraid you're too late. He turned himself into a cat's dinner and he's halfway down my tum by now. (*He rubs his stomach happily*)
Gruesome (*startled*) What? Then I must fly. (*He turns to leave* R)

Jack enters DR *with his sword drawn*

Jack I think not, Mr Gruesome.

Jack forces Gruesome back C

Marjory (*delightedly*) Jack.
Gruesome Very well. (*He turns rapidly to face Peter*) Then fight we shall. (*He lunges at Peter*)

A fierce fight develops

Marjory hurries to Jack's side

All shout encouragement to Peter as the fight continues

At last Peter runs Gruesome through

   With a loud cry Gruesome staggers back and dies off stage

All cheer

   Mother Goose enters DR

Mother Goose (*beaming*) Well fought, young Master Peter
              Your destiny's fulfilled.
              With Puss's help, the day's been won . . .
              Both Crunchbones *and* his henchman killed.
              Now Ogre's castle, lands and gold
              Are yours by victor's right . . .
              Which means, without a doubt, your future
              Looks to be *extremely* bright.

All react with delight

              Yet ere you start to celebrate
              With all your happy friends . . .
              There's someone here, I think
              Who'd truly like to make amends (*She waves her spoon*)

   Caspar and Hector enter DL *cleaned up and looking shamefaced*

Caspar (*sniffling*) We're sorry for all the trouble we've caused. Trying to cheat you out of the will and kidnapping Marjory. You won't send us to prison or have our heads chopped off, will you?

Hector (*sniffling*) We'll never be naughty again—honest.

Peter Well—I suppose I should be furious, but if you hadn't done what you did, I'm sure none of this would have happened. And as things have turned out, I couldn't have asked for anything better of life, so we'll accept your apology and say no more about it.

Mother Goose (*beaming*) Then one last gift—for after this
              Our paths no longer cross . . .
              From this day on, your rank will be
              The *true* Marquis of Carabosse.

   Mother Goose exits DR

Everyone congratulates Peter

   The Chamberlain enters UR

Chamberlain (*loudly*) Her Royal Majesty, Queen Fanny the Fifth.

   The Queen and Freckles enter

Queen (*brightly*) Hallo, darlings. No wonder we couldn't find you. What on earth are you doing in the kitchen?

Peter We'll explain later, Your Majesty, but right now I'd like to ask for your daughter's hand in marriage.

Queen (*beaming*) Well, after looking around *this* place, I can't think of anyone I'd like her to marry more. It's big enough for a *giant* to live in. (*She chuckles*) Go on—take her. And I hope you'll both be as happy as me and Freckles are going to be.

Freckles looks askance at her

Peter (*delightedly*) Oh, I'm sure we *will* be. And we'll start the wedding preparations right away.

Freckles Then what are we waiting for? Get the champagne out and let's have a celebration.

All cheer

The Assistant Cooks enter with champagne bottles

Everyone joins in a rousing song of celebration to end the scene

Song 18 (Company)

Black-out

SCENE 6

An Anteroom in the castle. A lane scene

The Queen enters

Queen Oh, I say, girls and boys, isn't it exciting? There's going to be so many weddings round here in the next few days, we won't know whether we're coming or going. I mean, there's Peter and Miranda's today—Jack and Marjory's tomorrow morning—and mine and Freckles in the afternoon. The only thing is, they're all being held in different places and we haven't enough singers for all the choirs, so I just popped out here to see if you could help us? I'm sure you could, couldn't you?

Audience reaction

Come on. Don't be shy. Speak to Queenie. You could help us out, couldn't you?

Audience reaction

That's better. Now I've got a little song for us to practice with, so I'll sing it first, then you can all join in the second time and we'll see what sort of noise you can make.

The Queen does the Song Sheet

Right. Now it's your turn.

The audience sing through

(*Disappointed*) Well that wasn't very good, was it? I'm sure you can do better than *that*.

Freckles enters

Freckles What are you doing, Fanny? What was that horrible noise?

Queen Yes, it was a bit peculiar, wasn't it? I'm trying to get them singing the National Anthem, but they don't seem to have *got* it.

Freckles I don't know. There's a few out there got *something*. I think it must be indigestion. Here, I'll tell you what. Let's have another go. You take all the ladies and I'll take all the fellers.

The Queen and Freckles do the song sheet as required

At the end of the song, the Lights fade rapidly as:

The Queen and Freckles exit

SCENE 7

The Great Ballroom of the castle. Brightly lit

Full set. There is a huge ballroom and staircase, with a backdrop of pillars and windows

If required, a lively dance may be inserted here. Following this, the walk-down commences in this fashion

> Babes
> Juniors
> Choristers
> Crunchbones (Performer carrying Ogre's head only)
> Chamberlain
> Jack and Marjory
> Gruesome
> Mother Goose
> Caspar and Hector
> Freckles and Queen
> Puss
> Peter and Princess

Peter Our fairy-tale is ended. Its course, the story's run.

Princess We hope we've entertained you with our dances, songs and fun.

Freckles But a warning as you leave us and file out into the street . . .

Queen Some dirty dog's been running loose. So watch where you put your feet. Good-night, everybody. (*She waves*) Good-night.

There is a reprise of any of the songs

CURTAIN

FURNITURE AND PROPERTY LIST

ACT I

Prologue

Personal: **Mother Goose:** wooden spoon

Scene 1

On stage: Half-timbered cottages with thatched roofs
Small rustic bridge
Shops

Off stage: Scroll **(Chamberlain)**

Personal: **Peter:** stick and bundle
Gruesome: coiled whip
Queen: glittering crown
Chamberlain: rod of office

Scene 2

Personal: **Gruesome:** belt and will

Scene 3

On stage: Fortune teller's tent or caravan
Stalls
Trees

Off stage: Red boots **(Mother Goose)**
Peter's stick and bundle **(Freckles)**

Personal: **Chamberlain:** Rod of office
Princess: tiara
Mother Goose: wooden spoon
Puss: cat mask

Scene 4

Off stage: Sack **(Puss)**

Personal: **Gruesome:** belt and will
Puss: belt and dagger

Scene 5

On stage: Trees
Thick shrubs
Signpost to lake (R) and to Arcadia (L)
Rolled towels
Picnic baskets

Off stage: **Peter's** clothes in a bundle **(Puss)**

ACT II

Scene 1

On stage: Beautiful garden with flowering shrubs, etc.
Fountains
Statues
White painted garden bench
Graceful trees

Scene 2

Personal: **Mother Goose:** wooden spoon

Scene 3

On stage: Arch
Courtyard
Buttress

Personal: **Ogre:** wooden staff
Peter: sword
Jack: sword

Scene 4

On stage: Nil

Scene 5

On stage: Kitchen table. *On it:* pastry bowl. *In it:* artificial "dumplings", a bag of
flour, mixing spoon, box of eggs. *On the side of the table:* fly-swat and
large frying pan, plant pot. *In it:* artificial flowers

Off stage: Soda syphon **(Hector)**
Trayful of large shaving mousse pies on paper plates **(Chamberlain)**
Flagon of wine **(Gruesome)**
Boot **(Medium-sized fish)**
Mallet **(Octopus)**

Personal: **Caspar:** moustache
Hector: moustache
Mother Goose: wooden spoon
Peter: sword
Jack: sword
Gruesome: sword

LIGHTING PLOT

ACT I

Various interior and exterior settings

PROLOGUE

To open: Early morning effect

Cue 1   **Mother Goose** flourishes her spoon   (Page 2)
           Flash

ACT I

To open   Bright sunny effect

Cue 2   Everyone exits miserably   (Page 7)
           Lights dim

Cue 3   **Mother Goose:** "... walking Puss in Boots"   (Page 12)
           Black-out. When ready, bring up bright sunny effect downstage

Cue 4   **The Babes** dance off with **Freckles** at the end of the song   (Page 14)
           Rapid fade to Black-out. When ready, bring up bright sunny
             effect

Cue 5   **Puss** and **Peter** exit   (Page 20)
           Black-out. When ready, bring up general exterior lighting

Cue 6   **Puss** exits, laughing delightedly   (Page 23)
           Black-out. When ready, bring up general exterior lighting

ACT II

To open: Sunny day effect

Cue 7   **Gruesome** drags the struggling **Princess** off DL, roaring with   (Page 34)
             laughter
           Rapid fade to black-out. When ready, bring up daylight effect

Cue 8   **Puss** exits L brightly   (Page 37)
           Fade to Black-out. When ready, bring up early evening effect

Cue 9   At the end of the song **Freckles** and the **Queen** exit DL   (Page 42)
           Rapid fade to Black-out. When ready, bring up dim, gloomy
             exterior effect

Cue 10   **The Monster** screams and exits   (Page 46)
           Black-out. When ready, bring up very gloomy, dim interior effect

Cue 11   **Ogre:** "Hokus-pokus, fiddle-de-dum . . ."   (Page 51)
            Lights fade to a total black-out by the end of the spell

Cue 12   Eerie music begins to play   (Page 51)
            Change to U.V. lighting

Cue 13   The stage is empty once more   (Page 52)
            Lights return to very dim and gloomy with U.V. on

Cue 14   **Ogre:** "Via Germanicus, dabbicus AYE."   (Page 52)
            Lights fade to black-out

Cue 15   **Ogre:** "Let there be light then."   (Page 53)
            Lights return to original state but the U.V. switches off

Cue 16   At the end of song 18   (Page 55)
            Black-out. When ready, bring up general lighting downstage

Cue 17   The **Queen** and **Freckles** exit   (Page 56)
            Fade rapidly to black-out. When ready, bring up general lighting

EFFECTS PLOT

PROLOGUE

MADE AND PRINTED IN GREAT BRITAIN BY
LATIMER TREND & COMPANY LTD PLYMOUTH
MADE IN ENGLAND